REMEMBERING MY ROOTS
Through
FOOD, CULTURE
and LANGUAGE

Harriet M. Reiss

PublishAmerica
Baltimore

First printing

At the specific preference of the author, PublishAmerica allowed this work to remain exactly as the author intended, verbatim, without editorial input.

ISBN: 1-4241-4800-6
PUBLISHED BY PUBLISHAMERICA, LLLP
www.publishamerica.com
Baltimore

Printed in the United States of America

WITH LOVE
TO ALL MY FAMILY

TABLE OF CONTENTS

FAMILY RECIPE INDEX

ACKNOWLEDGMENTS

I wish to acknowledge my two readers who provided helpful suggestions for this book: my husband Ira who spent hours scanning photos and documents for the book, advising me on computer software and more—and then reading the final copy—thank you, Ira for your enormous help. And to my good friend Marcia Hinitz, who could write her own book on her numerous foreign travels and her endless hours of volunteerism, I thank you for reading my book and for your suggestions on improving it.

Thanks also goes to my brother, Donald Eisman, my cousins Walter Winthrop, Myrna Kams Yunes and Harold Kams, Dorothy Pike and Florence Feldinger for their help in providing photos and/or information about family memories in the 1940's-1950's.

Lastly, I would like to thank all the staff at PublishAmerica for their professional help and expertise in the timely production of my book.

Chapter One
WHY I AM WRITING THIS BOOK

Yiddish, Food and Culture

Yiddish is a language of humor and love, rich in idioms, color and expression. Among my extended family, English was heavily sprinkled with Yiddish. I understood it well but spoke it infrequently. In addition, speaking Yiddish when friends were around or in public was not cool for kids when I was growing up. In fact, as a teenager and even older I was embarrassed if my mother spoke Yiddish to me in public. I wanted her to speak English. My grandmothers spoke mostly Yiddish to me but they understood my English response. As a teen in the late 1940's and even beyond I wanted to assimilate into the general culture.

Now as I have just turned 72, I find I want to pass on the color and humor of the language and the culture to you, my children, your partners and my grandchildren and future generations. These are the readers for whom I first began to write this book. But as I wrote, I realized my story is one that all immigrant families experience. Whether from Russia, Mexico or Asia, families come with their customs and traditions and languages. And while continuing to value their own native traditions, their goal is to assimilate into American culture as they raise a new generation of Americans. And often it is the school children of these immigrants who bring home to their parents the new language of English.

Some of the stories you in my family will read here you already know—but you will see how the Yiddish language, the food and the culture of Jewish immigrants have helped shape our family. Others reading this book are far more informed than I on the traditions and rituals of Jewish life and some of you may be more Orthodox in your beliefs. I tell my story as I saw it and lived it and I hope my telling sheds a little bit of light on my family's culture, food and language.

Yiddish, you know, is actually a form of German heard centuries ago and is also a mix of Polish, Russian and other eastern European languages. Wherever eastern Jews emigrated to—Canada, New Zealand, Australia, Latin America, African countries, America, and of course Israel, they brought with them the Yiddish language.

Today some Yiddish words have become so universal that one sees words like *mensch* (a person respected for moral and ethical principles), or the useful word *schlep* (drag or carry or haul) and of course, *Shalom* (Peace) used frequently. The late Leo Rosten, Yiddish writer and humorist, remarked in his 2001 publication that he had been told there were some 500 Yiddish words in Webster's Unabridged Dictionary.

I recently read what Yiddish writer Isaac Bashevis Singer had to say about the language in his 1978 Nobel Prize for Literature acceptance speech: "Yiddish language…is a language of exile, without a land, without frontiers, not supported by any government, a language which possesses no words for weapons, ammunition, military exercises, war tactics…" I did not know this, and I was happy to read it.

The Yiddishisms (Yiddish words and expressions) you hear today are almost universal, but the language itself is disappearing. I think my parents' generation is the last of Jewish Americans to use Yiddish as the spoken language. According to Mickey Pearlman, reviewer of author Aaron Lansky's 2005 book Outwitting History, there were some 30,000 literary titles between 1864 and 1939, including Shakespeare, Tolstoy and Jack London that were translated into Yiddish. Today Jews around the world generally speak the language of their native land.

Yiddish and Hebrew are different languages. Yiddish is basically a spoken language but written Yiddish can use the English alphabet or the Hebrew alphabet. Yiddish also uses a great many Hebrew words, as most of you know, and as you shall see as you read on. Written Yiddish is read (like Hebrew) from right to left.

Interestingly, few Israelis speak Yiddish. In fact, Yiddish is rather ignored as a living language among most Israelis, according to the late Rosten's 2001 publication. Many native Israelis do not even know Yiddish. At any rate, the Eisman and Kamsky and Reiss families brought from their European homes to the United States their ancestral language of Yiddish in all its glory and you will see that in this book.

Yiddish—Wrapped Around a Blintz

So much of the Yiddish I heard was wrapped around food—a blintz, a knish, a matzo ball and more. As far back as I can remember family conversation in Yiddish and English, especially among the women in my family, often revolved around the cooking and serving of food. Whether it was to celebrate milestones like weddings or Bar Mitzvahs and Jewish holidays or sorrowful events like illness or death, the topic would be food: what would be cooked, who would prepare it and when would we eat it.

So food is everywhere in this story about my ancestors and my growing up in Boston. Also, here in my book you, my family, will find the traditional Jewish recipes you have asked for—all in one place. Some are from my mother, some from my Auntie Rose and others have a bit of modification here and there; and then there are my own recipes. Actually, my mother didn't write down a lot of her recipes; she cooked by tasting and after the dish was perfected, the recipe was in her head. My father used to joke she practically had a meal with all the tasting she did while cooking. I find I do a lot of that myself—a squirt of white wine here, a teaspoon of sugar there, a bit more garlic or other seasoning and so on until I have achieved the flavor I am looking for.

Today as I prepare these recipes, I often remember connections that I thought I had forgotten. I would guess that my children—David, Pam and Joel and their families, as well as other readers, will recall their own family traditions as they decide on a recipe to cook up for serving to loved ones. On Yom Kippur, slice up the apple, pour the honey for a sweet year, and pass it around the table. It's a simple ritual, but one our family has always done and, I think, will be repeated and remembered in the coming generations. And when you continue the tradition of family Seders, using our family Hagaddahs, you in my family, will see the familiar wine and juice stains on various pages that reflect the many happy years of Seders, and you will recall the laughter and banter around the table.

More Reasons for Writing This Book

There are other reasons for my writing this book. Much of my childhood experiences no longer exist, so remembering them and writing them down is useful for me as well as for future generations. With the passing of my mother, Sylvia Eisman in 2001, and the more recent passing of my Auntie Rose, the happy banter of Yiddish that I remember is fading from my own memory; so putting my story in writing helps me remember the language as well. You know, I actually learned a good deal about Judaism and the Yiddish language while researching and writing this book—and I made contact with relatives who then provided pictures and stories to make our family history more complete, and those people are thanked in my Acknowledgments in the beginning of this book.

Writing a Personal Account

Writing a personal history that others may read poses several challenges—the most important to me is that I not embarrass or upset anyone who may read this account. Thus, some more private events or matters may not be included.

My childhood was a simple one based on the traditions and customs of my parents' families and their ancestors. We did what we were told and didn't object or ask why. That was a different generation, you know, and a different time.

Things have certainly changed since I was a kid growing up in the mid 1930's and 1940's. Life seemed simpler—less rushed, less hectic. You knew what was expected of you and you followed the rules. And society enforced many of those rules. But looking back, one can see drawbacks. Why? Fixed rules do not typically encourage independent thinking. Today kids are freer to express their own views and opinions. Although this freedom—and certainly our media—can sometimes lead kids into undesirable friendships and directions, still I think independent thinking and free and open expression are important for a child's intellectual and emotional development. And I believe one can express one's views, openly and freely (in most situations) while still respecting others. This **respect** for others I think is a key to better relations—in our personal lives as well as in our broader society. No matter our skin color, religion, age, ethnic background or sexual orientation, talking about issues **respectfully** and **kindly** can make a difference. Words may sometimes hurt but they can also explain and heal.

Lastly, I am writing this book for Jews and non-Jews alike who have or may join our extended family—as well as other readers—so they can see from whence we came, and hopefully where I hope we can go to make our planet a better and safer place for all.

My book is a tale of growing up in Boston in the 1930's up until 1955 and my story ends when I leave my parents' home at age 21 after I married. So the focus here is on my family's ancestors and the impact their food and culture and language had on their lives both in Russia and America and how the Great Depression and World War II affected our lives as I was growing up. There is certainly much more to tell after 1955. My life has been full and rich and my experiences abundant. Seeing you, my children—David, Pam and Joel—grow up to become wonderful, productive, smart, and kind adults has brought me great joy, and my life with Dad, though rocky at times, has been fulfilling and happy. And to my grandkids—Sam, Max, Jake, Joey and Rachel—you make me proud everyday with everything that you know and do for yourselves and for others. Keep up the excellence in all that you do— schoolwork, music, athletics—and try to extend kindness to all people you meet to help make this a better world for ourselves and for others. Try to be a role model for your friends by embracing diversity. Talk it up. Invite new immigrant kids to hang out with you.

Sadly, my parents, Grandma and Grandpa Eisman are no longer here to read this story. It never occurred to me while my mother was still living to do such a book—and I am sorry that I did not think of it back then. Luckily though, in the early 1980's while sitting by a pool in Florida, my mother and I did write up genealogy charts of both the Eisman and Kamsky families, and a lot of the information you read here comes from that long weekend.

Both my parents would have appreciated this book—I am sure they would be proud of their family's accomplishments. We are all products of our ancestors—a little bit of Kamsky and Eisman and Reiss reside in each one of us in our family. Lastly, my parents would be happy to know that I am preserving, in writing, their culture and language that was so predominant in my family roots.

Actually, I started this process intending to write down a few Yiddish expressions and translations, a bit about my parents' background and a few traditional family recipes. After taking a short memoirs' writing workshop, I expanded my plan to include more about my family's culture and my upbringing in Boston as well as my strong feelings on social justice and equality. Never did I dream my "brief family story" would take so much time and lots of computer education to become the manuscript you are now reading.

Onto a few remaining items in the book. You will find that my Yiddish words and phrases, and Hebrew words as well, are in *italics* and the English translation following is in parenthesis. Genealogy Charts are at the end of Chapter Four; and photos, documents and other memorabilia are in the Photo Section following Chapter Ten. The Family Recipe Index is located in the last part of the Table of Contents.

Tic/Tac/Toe Fun

At the close of each chapter (except the last), you will find an abstract Tic/ Tac/Toe icon with a letter marked in each icon. Follow them through, and you will spell out three words that are very important for all of us. I first did this tic/tac/toe feature because at the time I began writing this book, my granddaughter Rachel, about eight at the time, and I often played tic/tac/toe. And so I continued this abstract bit for my grandkids even when I decided to publish the book. Do check them out; they are easy, fun and important.

A Word About the Spelling of Yiddish Words

You frequently see Yiddish words spelled several different ways. All are correct, it seems. Even the word for grandmother can be seen spelled *Bubby, Bubbe* or *Bobie*. When I was growing up, notes or letters to or about my grandmother were written "Dear *Bobby*" so I thought my family had been misspelling *Bubbe's* name for years. Flash forwarding to probably 1993 on Grandma Eisman's birthday: When Grandma first saw the towel David and Sue had given her "To *Bubbe*, from Sam and Max," she whispered to me: "They misspelled *Bubbe!*" Recently I consulted the late Leo Rosten's book for clarification and to my amazement, he too wrote about his *"Bobby." Chuppah* (bridal canopy with four poles which symbolizes the home) can be seen spelled *Chuppa* and *Chupeh*. Hebrew words likewise have different spellings in English and it seems all are correct. I have always spelled the Festival of Lights *Chanukah*; it is often seen as *Hanukah or Hanukkah*. And there are a great many more Yiddish words with various spellings one sees in the literature, greeting cards and elsewhere. Pronunciations differ depending on the area of Europe from which a family has emigrated. The pronunciations you read here are the ones with which I grew up.

Okay, while you, my children—David, Pam and Joel—were growing up in the Midwest, you remember that Dad and I rarely spoke Yiddish in our home. Your grandparents lived far away in Boston, New York and Scranton; thus, you heard Yiddish being spoken only on visits with your grandparents. When Pam one day asked me what a *shmatteh* (rag) is, I knew I had to do this book. I must say though, in recent years, I do hear more Yiddishisms especially from Pam and Joel and that both pleases and amuses me.

To prepare for the writing of this book, I looked through old pictures, letters, and family documents, and some are included here. I listened to audiotapes of my parents and my Auntie Rose describing their native Russia and their experiences coming to the United States. And I wrote to and talked with relatives to get information.

So, here goes—with a little humor and a lot of love to you all— David and Sue, Pam and Brian and Joel and my grandkids, Sam, Max,

Jake, Joey and Rachel and to future generations as well as other readers, I will tell my story.

_P_/___/____
__/__/__
/   /

Chapter Two
LIFE in RUSSIA in the EARLY 1900's

Homage to My Parents, Sam and Sylvia Eisman

I want to begin by paying homage here to my parents—*alevhasholem (*may they rest in peace)—this expression is common and pays respect for the departed. So I pay homage here to my parents for their efforts and hard work, especially during the depression when jobs were hard to come by and times were tough. My parents were first generation Americans who worked hard to make a living and to integrate into their new culture. When they married in 1931 during the depression years, there were some fine times but many struggles for them as well as you will see.

The Early 1900's in Russia

My parents did not know each other in Russia but both lived in the Ukraine—each in a *shtetl* (small town or village where Jewish families lived)—my father from Zhytomyr and my mother from Chernigov—both big cities today. It was the custom and the necessity at the time that the husband/father would go to America ahead of the rest of the family to relatives who could sponsor and help him find work. Later the remainder of the family would follow after the father had found work and a place for them to stay as well as enough money to pay for their travel to America. Often many years separated fathers from their families. In my mother's family her father, *Zeyde* (grandfather) Kamsky had left for America in 1913 and was gone for almost 9 years before the family joined him in Boston. Actually my *Zeyde* Kamsky did have the money and papers arranged for their travel to America at an earlier time, but my *Bubbe* Kamsky refused to leave until her older sons had completed their military service in World War I and could go with them. As it turned out, by then they had married and decided to stay in Russia.

My Grandfather's Out-of-Marriage Love Hurts the Family

In my father's case, his father had left Russia around 1910 with his oldest daughter, Becky, and he was gone for almost 12 years. (When I questioned my father years ago as to why my grandfather did not take Koppel, the oldest son with him to America which was the custom at the time, my father thought for a while and said he did not know.)

Without a family in America, my paternal grandfather became involved with another woman and some years later returned to Russia, "arriving in the middle of the night," my mother later told me, to ask his wife, my grandmother for a divorce. "She threw him out of the house," my mother said, and he was never really close to the family again. However, I remember my parents helping him out once or twice during my childhood plus allowing him to live with us for a short time when things were tough for him.

My father at one time went to my grandfather's woman and asked her to give up my grandfather. She refused saying something like "You love your father—well, I love him too." This affair was never discussed in my family. My father was very private about such family matters and I guess did not want us to know about this relationship. I was quite grown when my mother told me about this affair—it is now time for the story to be aired. I did know my paternal *Zeyde* Eisman—I remember his occasional visits to our home; he was always dapper and smiled easily. But his visits were brief—the whole extended family was saddened by this extramarital affair. My grandmother never agreed to the divorce my grandfather wanted.

Great Tragedy in the Shtetl

In the *shtetls* in Russia where both my parents' families had lived, Jews were usually poor and restricted to these areas by the Tsarist government, thus isolated from the rest of Europe. Harshly discriminated against during this time (early 1900's), and often assaulted during the pogroms (attacks by anti-Semitic and anti-Bolshevik thugs), these actions were tolerated or ignored and even condoned by government officials. It was in this cruel climate that my mother's older brother, Doddle, about 16 at the time was brutally beaten by these bandits while my grandmother pleaded on her knees for them to stop. Terrified, Doddle's siblings stood by, unable to stop this horrible attack. Tragically, Doddle died from this beating within months. Tearfully and sadly—so sadly, my mother and grandmother lifted his body onto a sled and took him to the cold countryside for burial. This tragedy in 1917 happened during the years my mother's father was in America, so it was doubly difficult for my mother's family to endure his terrible death.

While my paternal grandfather was in America, my paternal grandmother, my father and his siblings, Auntie Molly and Uncle Izzy lived with their grandmother Dvorah. Dvorah was a woman with strong convictions. In the early 1900's, as I said, pogroms were occurring frequently in the shtetl in my father's village as well. Anti-Semitic hoodlums would bang on the doors of the villagers and order the occupants to leave whereupon valuables were stolen or trashed. The terrified families would run into the hills to hide until it was safe to return. When my great grandmother Dvorah refused to leave her home on one of these pogrom attacks, tragically, she was shot and killed. So my parents, although they did not know each other in the Ukraine, suffered intolerably in this anti-Semitic climate, both losing members of their family who were killed during these pogroms. See photos of my father, his siblings and my paternal grandmother, *Bubbe* Frieda Eisman and great grandmother Dvorah in the beginning pages of the Photo Section following Chapter Ten.

So you can see why my parents' families wanted to escape from the anti-Semitic and often unsafe living conditions in their homeland.

They wanted to come to America for religious freedom and economic opportunities for themselves and their children.

Chapter Three
HAPPIER TIMES and
MORE STORIES from RUSSIA

Zeyde Kamsky Makes His Pickles and Jams

There were also happy times in Russia around 1910 or so with family rituals and celebrations. My maternal grandfather liked pickling apples and cucumbers and making jam. He cooked the strawberry and raspberry fruit outside in an open fire while neighborhood children gathered around holding their piece of bread as they waited for their dollop of jam. My mother and her siblings loved their father's easy smile and his devotion to his family.

So my mother, and her sister, my Auntie Rose waited with the rest of the neighborhood children for their father's jam to be cooked. The two older brothers, Nomi and Schnaer, helped in the jam making effort—the local girls hanging on Nomi's every word. All the neighborhood girls liked Nomi, my mother had told me, because he was fun to be with and handsome too.

My mother adored her father who was a chimneysweeper in Russia and in America ran a fruit store, first in Revere and then in Dorchester. He and my grandmother were very much in love and had eloped because my grandmother's older sister was not yet married and it was customary for the older daughter to marry first. This caused great conflict in the family, and my grandmother and her new husband moved from Chernigov to another town. My grandmother never received her dowry of pillows that was the customary gift from the bride's parents to the newly married couple at the time. So my mother and her older siblings were born in Ekaterinoslav in northern Ukraine. Later the families reunited and returned to Chernigov where my Auntie Rose and Uncle Irving were born. My *Bubbe* Kamsky had seven children; one died in infancy.

The Eismans and the Appotives

My father, his siblings and their mother, my paternal *Bubbe* lived in the same *shtetl* as their Auntie Surah and Uncle Avraham Appotive and their four sons, Rudy, Dave, Joe and Benny. The families were very close, and my father talked often of the love and affection and attention he and his siblings received from his Auntie Surah and Uncle Avraham, especially during the years my paternal grandfather was in America. He told us of the closeness he felt for them and their sons. The Appotives later settled in Canada—in Ottawa and Montreal—and my parents kept in close touch with them over the years.

So after my paternal *Zeyde* Eisman left Russia for what had been his second journey back to America, my father and his siblings—sister Molly and brothers, Izzy and Koppel—lived with their mother and helped her in every way they could. Sadly, Koppel, the oldest son was killed in 1918 during World War I. My *Bubbe* Frieda Eisman (your great grandmother) had seven children; she, like my *Bubbe* Breina Kamsky, had a child who died in infancy.

So my parents and their families suffered through two wars in their young lifetimes—first in World War I when the Russians fought against the Germans. Then the Russians withdrew their military from World War I in 1917 because they needed the troops to fight in the Bolshevik Revolution, the civil war in their own country.

Bartering in Russia and a Near Fatal Accident

Bartering was common in Russia during the early 1900's when my parents were young. It was at such a time when my Auntie Rose and my mother, both under 10 were taking fabric dyes to a distant neighbor lady across the river who would in turn give them flour for baking bread.

It was early springtime and the river was starting to thaw. Still they trudged with their sled across the melting ice, only to find that they and their sled and their bundles going under. Villagers looked in horror thinking they would drown but luckily they made it across, soaked but alive and taken in to dry out and be fed. This is a story that I remember way back as a kid. My Auntie Rose remembers this experience with great amusement, but my mother, the older and more cautious of the two, said she cried and worried how they would return home. There had been a lot of snow that winter and the melting had caused the river to overflow so there was much anxiety in the region. Still, the next day a villager was able to accompany the two sisters around the river and they arrived home safely.

Grandma Eisman, Auntie Rose and the Plum Orchard

My mother's family lived near a fruit orchard. One day my Auntie Rose spotted some beautiful plums hanging from the plum tree. She encouraged my mother to climb over the fence with her to pick some beauties. My Auntie Rose had just scaled the fence and was putting the plums into her full skirt when the owner, whip in hand, spotted them and began running after them. Both kids raced off and outran the owner. The fruit was brought to their mother who cooked some and sold some at the local fruit market. Your Grandma Sylvia Eisman and your Great Auntie Rose never again ventured into this fruit orchard.

My Mother's Lockjaw: She Is Critically Ill

The wedding celebration in 1915 of my mother's brother and his new wife was a joyous occasion for the whole family in Russia. In the excitement of serving up food to the family, my mother, barefoot on a wooden floor, got a big splinter in her foot. (She actually described it as a big piece of wood.) Though the family tried to remove it, they could not and after a couple of soakings I guess they assumed the splinter would fall out. It was a few weeks later that my mother became very ill with lockjaw (tetanus), a serious and acute infection, from the dirty wood "that had traveled through her body," my mother would later tell us.

The disease is called lockjaw because difficulty in opening one's mouth is often the first symptom of it; hence the "locked jaw"—which literally becomes locked in place. There were no tetanus shots in Russia at that time and the infection almost killed my mother. She was hospitalized and sick for many months. Spiritual healers brought in by my grandparents were of no avail.

Slowly, she began to recover. The wood had traveled through her body and came out of her hip many months after! Doctor friends have told me a thick splinter traveling through a person's body would indeed be rare but could happen. My mother has said a Russian doctor had told her if she survived tetanus, she would survive anything. She often repeated this over the years through her many illnesses and surgeries. My mother lived to be 95 years old.

_/__/__
_/__/_
/A /

Chapter Four
COMING to AMERICA: THE EARLY YEARS in the 1920's and BEYOND

Preparing for the Big Move to the United States: The Kamskys' Departure

There were many stories of my mother and her family's excursion to America. From their home city of Chernigov they traveled to Moscow. My *Bubbe* Kamsky wanted to spend time with sons Nomi and Schnaer who were now married and, as I said earlier, had decided to remain in Russia. So *Bubbe* Kamsky and my mother and her siblings stayed on for a few months in Nomi's wife's mother's home. Impoverished as they all were, my *Bubbe* bartered various possessions—her big clock, for example—that were exchanged for flour so she could bake bread for her family.

Later in Moscow they lived for a time in an old school with other immigrants who were also awaiting departure to America. In the next room lived a prostitute who brought her customers into her room to conduct business. My mother and my Auntie Rose discovered a small hole in the wall, and there they witnessed the prostitute at work. Grandma Eisman and my Auntie Rose gave their account of this story with great amusement.

Also in Moscow, my mother and my Auntie Rose told us, "We were selling cigarettes to make some money but because we were under age, we were arrested and sent to jail. Since we were both under 16, we started crying, so after two hours they let us go." This was told with great laughter.

The Kamskys Make the Journey to America

After some months and tears of sadness because brothers Nomi and Schnaer were not traveling to the new country, the family boarded a smaller boat to Liverpool, England where they would depart for America. Their youngest sibling, my Uncle Irving, was about 12 at the time; years later in Boston he would become a high school music teacher and great musician playing saxophone and clarinet with well-known bands. Brother Schnaer who stayed in Russia played the mandolin and later a violin. So you see I passed some musical genes down to you—my kids and grandkids! See photos of Schnaer playing the mandolin and later the violin—and also look in the Photo Section for my Uncle Irving with his saxophone.

After many days in Liverpool, they were finally able to board the "Berengaria," the ship that would take them to America. Traveling across the vast Atlantic Ocean to America, my *Bubbe* Kamsky was asked by ship officials to help other families—to scrub the hair and scalp and remove lice from other children's hair because if skin diseases or eruptions were present, they would not be allowed off the ship. This was a *mitzvah (a* kind deed to help others) and my grandmother was more than happy to help the many families that were in need.

The Goldene Landt (The Golden Land)

Coming to America—the goldene landt *(golden land)* was a dream come true for both my parents and their families as it was for so many immigrants. My parents both came to our country in 1922 when they were in their teens. My mother's excitement was enormous, she recalled, when she first saw the Statue of Liberty. Following are the words that were penned in 1883 by Emma Lazarus, the American Jewish poet in her ode to the Statue of Liberty. These words bid a welcome to the thousands of weary immigrants who came to America for religious freedom and economic opportunity.

"Give me your tired, your poor
Your huddled masses yearning to breathe free,
The wretched refuse of your teeming shore,
Send these, the homeless, tempest-tost (sic) to me,
I lift my lamp beside the golden door."

The organization HIAS (Hebrew Immigration Aid Society) helped my parents and their families as well as many other new immigrants when they arrived on Ellis Island in New York City. HIAS helped to facilitate legal entry and provide immediate care—food, shelter and comfort to new families. Immigration to the U.S. at that time was based on family and relatives and/or employment in America.

So there awaiting their arrival was my maternal grandfather *Zeyde* Kamsky who had left Russia nine years earlier. Finally, at long last, his family had come to America. He was overjoyed, as was all the family as they hugged and kissed staring in disbelief that they were now together. My Auntie Rose tells me her first thought when she saw her "Pa," as he was called, was "Gee…he's good looking." *Zeyde* Kamsky had brought bananas and other fruit for his arriving family. His children had never seen bananas in Russia and he watched as they peeled and ate the fruit, saying to his wife "Our children know how to survive…they will be alright."

The Eismans Make the Journey to America

Meanwhile, Grandpa Eisman and his siblings and their mother, my paternal *Bubbe* Frieda Eisman traveled from their home city of Zhitomyr, packing up their few household belongings for the trip to America. Pillows and bedding stuffed with feathers were in great demand in America, they had been told, and so my paternal *Bubbe* was sure to pack their precious bedding to try to sell in America. (Unfortunately, these feathers that they had carefully carried to the U.S. were not in demand—but they held on to their valuable bedding that, later you will see, was put to good use.) They too arrived at Ellis Island in 1922 to be met by HIAS who facilitated their arrival and provided necessary immediate care. They then prepared for their train ride to

Boston where they were met by relatives with whom they would temporarily live.

There were many immigrants from all over Europe who arrived at Ellis Island and were helped by HIAS. Some familiar names are the Broadway Legend Al Jolson who arrived from Lithuania, former Secretary of State Henry Kissinger from Germany and comedienne Joan Rivers' family who emigrated from Russia. Like all immigrants, Nobel Prize winner Thomas Mann, from Germany also arrived at Ellis Island.

The United States is, after all, a nation of immigrants. This is our heritage. Every day we open our arms and our shores to many of those in need of safety and survival. And you know what?—this pays off in big dividends. Why? People from other lands bring their cultures, their customs, their styles and their languages and we learn from them about our world. And then these immigrants study and learn our language, work at their jobs and pay their income taxes.

Immigration Today: No Easy Answers

Immigration in our country today is a complicated and difficult issue. Many people entering the United States come with no passport or visa or documents to show they may legally work and live here. A lot of these individuals find work that is not available in their own land; some work to send money back to their families in their native land to feed their children. Some people argue that illegal citizens take jobs that could go to Americans. Others say Americans don't want the jobs of picking crops, cleaning office buildings and bathrooms and working in nursing homes, so these illegal citizens are useful to our economy. And then some feel we need greater security so aliens cannot cross our border—that we may need a wall to protect us. Employers who hire new workers also have the responsibility to check the status and background of these potential workers to protect themselves and others from illegal aliens. And of course, there are many Europeans and others from around the world who have legally applied for emigration to the U.S. and wait years to come here.

How should we handle these complicated issues? To allow those illegal citizens already here obtain work permits for their temporary time in America and then get in line behind those who have been waiting legally to emigrate and become U.S. citizens may be one solution. I don't know what the fair solutions are to these difficult questions, but I hope our political leaders can find a way out of this crisis. One thing I do believe is that we Americans can and should welcome those from other countries into our neighborhoods, at our worksites, at the shopping malls. Isn't that how we would like to be treated if the situation were reversed? Wouldn't we want the tolerance, the acceptance and the smile at the grocery store?

Arriving in Boston

But I am getting away from my own family story in the early 1920's. As I mentioned earlier, my parents did not know each other in Russia, but both Sam Eisman and Sylvia Kamsky and their families settled in the Boston area in 1922 to begin their new lives. It was not easy to come to a new country and learn a new language. Take a look at the Russian phrases in the Photo Section. This alphabet is strange to us just as the English alphabet was to my parents and their families upon their arrival in America and just as it is today for the many new immigrants coming to America.

David, Pam and Joel (my kids)—remember our attempts, though often humorous, in translating and speaking the Swedish language during 1975-76, the year we spent in Sweden on Dad's Sabbatical? And don't forget English was a second language for many Swedes. Not so for the Russians who came to the United States in the 1920's. And the Russian language was a totally foreign tongue to English-speaking Americans.

But the Eismans and the Kamskys were excited to learn the language of their new homeland—and learn they did and adjust they did to their new world. A whole new culture awaited them—new currency, new customs, and more. I recently listened to some old tapes where my mother said she and her siblings did not speak Yiddish in their native land. Although they heard and understood Yiddish, they

35

responded in Russian. Only after coming to America, my mother said on our family tape, did she and her siblings begin talking routinely in Yiddish. I did not know this. As a kid, I remember my parents speaking Russian to each other when they did not want us to know a private matter—maybe related to sex or money or family gossip.

One language characteristic that I found interesting was the feminine and masculine name difference. In the Russian language women add "skaya" to their family name. So Kamsky became Kamskyskaya for my mother, her sister, and of course, my *Bubbe* Breina Kamskyskaya. Men simply went by the name Kamsky. When my mother talked about the feminine "skaya," she often smiled. I think she thought the sound was kind of musical plus I think it reminded her of the happy childhood years before her father had left for America. Wanting to assimilate quickly into American culture when they emigrated from the old country, the "skaya" was immediately dropped. And, of course, the same was true for my father's mother and her daughters.

Some of my mother's family was already in Boston, and her Auntie Razel, who was the oldest sister, helped the Russian relatives as they arrived. Razel was smart but she was controlling too. When her youngest and most beautiful sister, Etel had a proposal of marriage to a young man whom she wasn't sure she wanted to marry, Razel told her: "In America parents and elders are in charge. If parents aren't here, then you listen to your older sister (that was Razel) or else you go back to the old country!" Thus was Razel able to convince Etel to marry Yissa. I remember my great Aunt Etel and I liked her. She always smiled and was kind and it appeared she was happy in her marriage.

I remember another Great Aunt who the family called "the Gypsy" because she told people's fortunes, and some family members actually relied on her for answers to their problems. Great Aunt Rachel, her hair dyed a reddish-brown, dressed in bright colors and wore long fringed scarves. She was a colorful member of the family and was fun to be around.

Settling in: A New Culture

My mother often told me stories of missing Russia. She was 18 when she came to America and loved to read, so her father would get her Russian language novels at the public library. Her younger siblings were enrolled in public school, but being the oldest of the children in America, my mother had to go to work to help support the family. And so her English language learning was done in night school. My father, Grandpa Eisman, the youngest in his family at age 19 when he came to the United States, never attended day school because there was little money in his family, so it was necessary for him to work as well. His father who was a shoemaker, and as said earlier, had been involved with his outside-of-marriage love had never really supported his family. So Grandpa Eisman learned English in night school and that is where my parents met.

Who's Who? Genealogy Charts

Genealogy Charts follow this chapter to help you identify the people I talk about.

Frank and Frieda Eisman, my paternal grandparents;
Harry and Breina Kamsky, my maternal grandparents and
Samuel and Sylvia Eisman, my parents.

Although only three generations are shown on the Frank and Frieda Eisman genealogy chart—here is more: My *Bubbe* Frieda Eisman was one of three children. Her mother Dvorah, whom I mentioned earlier, was my great grandmother who was tragically shot and killed by anti-Jewish and anti-Bolshevik mobs during the pogroms of the early 1900's. My folks often talked about Grandpa Eisman's great grandfather Rudolph who lived to be 114 years old. That's the *emmes* (truth)! Grandpa Eisman said Rudolph had a second Bar Mitzvah at age 113! My records show Rudolph, who was my great great grandfather, was born around 1810 and died in 1924!

Only three generations are shown on the Harry and Breina Kamsky genealogy chart as well, but here's more: My *Bubbe* Kamsky was one of six children. Her mother's first husband Willwell (or Velvil) died

37

young and my great grandmother Bussie remarried Schmuel Fox who had lost a leg in an earlier war. Bussie and Schmuel had three children making a total of six children born to my great grandmother, Bussie Fox.

In recent years the Appotive family in Canada, close cousins to my father, if you remember, has located more extended family that had moved to Israel from Zhitomyr in the Ukraine where my father was born. A few years ago several of the Appotives traveled to Israel to meet these cousins and have since kept in touch. On my mother's side, my cousin Walter and I are communicating with other Kamsky people from the Ukraine to determine if there is any relation in our respective families. So the search goes on for distant relatives.

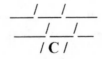

FRANK AND FRIEDA EISMAN FAMILY GENEALOGY

Frank Eisman
Born: 1877
Died: 1953
Shoe Repair Work
Came to U.S. with daughter Becky 1912

Frieda Appotive Eisman
Born: 1880
Died: 1947
Had severe limp
Came to U.S. 1922 with 3 remaining children

Becky Eisman
B: 1894
D: 1970
Heart Attack
M: Ely Lerman
Furniture Store

No Children

Molly Eisman
B: 1898
D: 1976
Lung Cancer
Seamstress in Factory
M: Max Margulis

Dorothy
Murray
Reuben

Koppel Eisman
B: 1899
D: 1917

Koppel Eisman died fighting with Bolsheviks against Mensheviks in Russian Revolution of 1917

Izzy Eisman
B: 1901
D: 1991
Upholsterer
M: Millie

Florence
Charlotte

Sam Eisman
B: 1903
D: 1981
Heart Attack
Upholsterer/
Owned Upholstering Shop
M: Sylvia Kamsky

Don
Harriet

Youngest Sibling
Died Young from illness
Did not come to U.S.

HARRY AND BREINA KAMSKY FAMILY GENEALOGY

Harry Kamsky
Born: 1871
Died: 1934
Stroke at age 62
Chimney Sweeper in Russia
Had fruit store in Revere & Dorchester
Came to U.S. in 1913

Breina Fox Kamsky
Born: 1877
Died: 1972
Had 2 hip surgeries and pacemaker
Came to US in 1922 with children

Nomi Kamsky
B: 1897
D: 1944
Killed in WW II
M: Maruzi
Did not go to U.S.
Nomi was barber

Schnaer Kamsky
B: 1899
D: unknown
M: she died from typhoid in epidemic;
M: 1st cousin Henke
Did not come to U.S.
Schnaer was officer in Russian government

Doddle Kamsky
B: 1901
D: 1917 (age 16)
Killed in pogrom by anti-Bolshevik/Anti-Semitic mob

Sylvia Kamsky Eisman
B: 1905
D: 2001
M: Sam Eisman 1931
Sylvia Lockjaw age 10

Rose Kamsky Kramer
B: 1907
D: 2003
M: Joe Winthrop who died in 1953
M: Morris Kramer

Irving Kams
B: 1911
D: 1978
Brain Cancer
M: Jeanette
Music teacher & Musician

(Schnaer's children)
Leyna, Son
Itzik
From first marriage
Henke from second marriage

(Sylvia's children)
Don
Harriet

(Rose's children)
Jerry
Walter

(Irving's children)
Harold
Billy
Myrna

A child born to Harry and Breina Kamsky after Doddle and before Sylvia died in infancy. Her name was Henke.

SAM AND SYLVIA EISMAN GENEALOGY

Although my family history in this book ends at the time I married in 1955, I'd like to present my husband Ira, my children and my grandchildren, along with my parents and my brother, Don, in this genealogy chart.

Sam Eisman
Born: 1903
Died: 1981
Upholsterer/Owner
American Upholstering Co.

Sylvia Eisman
Born: 1905
Died: 2001
Dressmaker and Homemaker

Donald Eisman

Born: 1932
Journalist
M: Mary Rogers
College Professor of Sociology

Harriet Eisman

Born: 1934
Homemaker, writer, corporate researcher, artist
M: Ira Reiss
College Professor of Sociology

(Note that both Don's spouse and Harriet's spouse are
College professors of Sociology)

David
B: 1959
Mgr., Operations & Technology
M: Sue Smoleroff, 1988
Mom, Marketing, Handicrafts

Pam
B: 1962
Mom, Social Worker
M: Brian Russ, 1990
Director, Teen Clinic

Joel
B: 1965
High School Math Teacher
Researcher/ Owner
Reiss Research

Sam Reiss
B: 12/17/90
Max Reiss
B: 5/27/92
Jacob Reiss
B: 5/4/97

Joseph Russ
B: 6/18/93
Rachel Russ
B: 11/24/95

41

Chapter Five
MY PARENTS' COURTSHIP and MARRIAGE

Learning English in Night School

It was in night school learning English that my parents met and courted, marrying in 1931. My father was "very funny and the life of the party," my mother later told us. "He often made me laugh and he was very good looking." My mother lived in Dorchester with her family, and my father lived in Revere with his family so it was a distance to travel even after my father bought his old car. So with a little persuasion, his mother agreed to move the family to Dorchester. My father, though the youngest child in the family, always seemed to carry a lot of weight in his family and with others as well. He was smart and assertive and honest and people listened to him. His family loved my mother who became very close with Auntie Molly, my father's sister. "She was a good woman; we were like sisters," my mother used to tell me.

All the women in both my parents' families—my Auntie Rose, my Auntie Molly and my mother worked as stitchers in the garment factories in Boston's Garment District—first when coming to America and then long after for necessary income. Co-workers at the garment factory where my mother had worked sewed her exquisite wedding dress shown in my parents' wedding photo in the Photo Section. Unfortunately, one or two years later, my mother's wedding dress was destroyed in a fire at her parents' home where my parents lived at the time.

Sam and Sylvia Eisman Marry

My parents were married in May of 1931 and honeymooned in Atlantic City, one of the popular honeymoon destinations in the early 1900's. Their wedding was just two years after the stock market crash and so I once asked my mother how they could afford such a lavish wedding at the time. She said she had saved every penny she could for many years especially for her dream wedding. Her parents did not have the money for a wedding so luckily she did. And at age 26 her dream came true. See my parents' wedding photo in the Photo Section.

After their marriage in 1931 and with little money, my parents found it necessary to live with my maternal grandparents until they were able to rent their own place. Later—still during the depression—my parents and my brother (I was not yet born) had to move back into *Bubbe* and *Zeyde* Kamsky's flat, joining my Auntie Rose Winthrop and her husband Joe and their family as well. Two young families living with their parents made for a very crowded household. But jobs were hard to get during the depression years so you stayed wherever you could to keep your family sheltered and fed.

Sadly, my mother's father died of a stroke in 1934 just three weeks before I was born. His name was Harry, and so I was named after him. My mother's family tried to keep his death from my mother since she was expecting me in three weeks but she said she knew he had died. Her last memory of her father, unable to speak because of the stroke, was of his lifting a frail finger to his cheek meaning he wanted a kiss from my mother. His death devastated my mother, as she was very close to her father.

Becoming American Citizens

It was with great pleasure when my parents received their American citizenship. In 1926 my mother, along with her siblings and her father, received their citizenship, then called the Certificate of Naturalization.

In 1922, the year my grandmother, *Bubbe* Kamsky, my mother and her siblings came to the U.S., a husband's naturalization or citizenship was no longer sufficient to make a wife a citizen; thus my maternal grandmother never became an American citizen. My father received his citizenship in 1929.

As I look at my father's photos as a young man, I see his famous signature was already taking shape. With one or two arm motions—almost as though he were going to paint on a canvas, he would sign his name—as would a calligrapher. See Samuel Eisman's "John Hancock" (signature) in the Photo Section.

My parents tried and mostly succeeded in assimilating into the American culture. But every so often my mother, recalling a particular incident, would say, "Well, what did we know? We were greenhorns!" (Newcomers—unfamiliar with ways of a new country). I thought for a long time this was my mother's own expression until one day years later I looked the word up in the dictionary—and there it was—plain as day.

As I became older, I began to understand more the experiences of my parents and their families in learning a new language, new currency, different dress styles and different foods. When newcomers are unfamiliar with American customs, they may act or do things in ways that are strange to us. Let's be curious but considerate about our new neighbors. Ask about them, respect them and invite them to join you in a basketball game, a picnic in the park or a movie. They want friendships just as we do; they want acceptance just as we do. So let's share our interests and our way of life with our newfound friends.

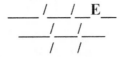

Where, after all, do universal human rights begin? In small places, close to home – so close and so small that they cannot be seen on any maps of the world...

Unless these rights have meaning there, they have little meaning anywhere.

— Eleanor Roosevelt

KIDS FLYING KITES, By Shirley V. Beckes
Reprinted by Permission of Getty Images 2006

Chapter Six
THE GREAT DEPRESSION
and its AFTERMATH

The 1929 Depression Disaster

The depression in 1929 caused a huge decline in the American economy. People lost their jobs, banks began closing and thousands lost their life savings. Great poverty and tragedy were common for many Americans. How would they feed their families and pay the rent? President Franklin Delano Roosevelt (FDR) became President in 1933 and almost immediately went into action with his New Deal. With the Congress, many social welfare programs and policies were enacted to get the economy moving again. These programs helped provide necessary jobs for many and helped to promote social and economic fairness and benefits for especially the poor and working class people. For example, the Wages and Hours Act was established as well as other measures to help working people. And Social Security was enacted and began in 1935.

FDR: "The Only Thing We Have to Fear is Fear Itself"

President Roosevelt's first Inaugural address in 1933 (one year before I was born) was one of the most significant inaugural addresses of our time. He talked of the country's suffering, and discussed ways he and Congress would put Americans back to work. "Our great nation will endure and revive and prosper..." he said, and then continued with his all-now famous statement: "The only thing we have to fear is fear itself." I recently looked back at his 1933 Inaugural Address when writing this book and found more in it that I liked. "Happiness lies not in the mere possession of money; it lies in the joy of achievement, in the thrill of the creative effort; we now realize" he went on…"our interdependence on each other…that we cannot merely take but we must give as well." Great stuff!

Luckily, in the 1930's my father found work through the Works Progress Administration (WPA) for $85.25 a month doing carpentry and helping to sew or hang draperies at theatres and other places in Boston. Work was sporadic but he took whatever he could get and was grateful for it. See his WPA Notice for Work in the Photo Section. My father was good at measuring, building and repairing and in establishing good working relationships.

Prior to the depression, Grandpa Eisman and my Uncle Izzy Eisman had made good use of the family's Russian bird feathers that I mentioned earlier when they began to work as upholsterers, stripping chairs and sofas and stuffing some with their precious Russian feathers that people asked for. Their efforts produced fine workmanship. Grandpa Eisman, on a tape I recently listened to, said he liked creating a sofa or chair from scratch rather than reupholstering them. Although most of his life's work was reupholstering furniture, it was quite an accomplishment to construct a piece of furniture from scratch, stuff it, stain and finish the wood and lay the fabric.

Grandpa Eisman's Upholstery Shop Gets Going

It was from his work with the Works Progress Administration that I mentioned earlier that Grandpa Eisman was able to move up into better paying jobs in upholstering—first working for others and eventually starting his own business in Melrose, Massachusetts in the mid to late forties. He named his business "American Upholstering Company." My kids, David and Sue have his glass sign hanging in their hallway—it is the same sign that hung for many years in the front window of his shop. The shop's slogan was "If It's American Made, It's Made Best." My father was proud to be an American citizen, and so he named his business and developed his slogan reflecting his pride.

Grandpa Eisman became a skilled and respected upholsterer, re-upholstering and making new furniture. Soon he was the main upholsterer for MIT, Tufts College, Eastern Airlines and private homes. His brother Izzy Eisman, also a skilled upholsterer, was a partner with him for a number of years; later my father also employed part-time upholsterers. Mrs. Florence Tyler was his bookkeeper through the 1940's and early 1950's, but in later years after I was married and gone and Mrs. Tyler retired, he did a lot of the office work himself, typing bills on his old Royal typewriter. Or when I visited, he'd ask me to type up statements, pay bills, file, etc.

Waiting for Our Sofa...

The old saying "the cobbler's children go barefoot" was apropos in our family. Some of our living room furniture spent months, even years, in my father's shop waiting to be reupholstered. This was a point of contention between my parents for as long as I can remember since my mother was anxious to get the sofa back and my father was too busy with customers' work to get it done. I never liked the tension caused by this. The sofa that David and Sue have was the same one in our living room when Don and I were little kids, under twelve years old and up, until the time I left home and got married. Dad and I courted on this sofa. So this sofa goes way back. My father used to have his *dremel* (nap) on this sofa in the earlier years.

Grandpa Eisman knew Boston well driving through the city and suburbs frequently to make house calls to pickup and deliver furniture. He knew every short cut in the city. Often he carried heavy chairs in and out of homes; we were always after him to get more help, but he chose to do a lot of it himself. Every once in a while he'd get home late and say he got *farblondzhet* (not just lost but really lost!). He worked hard but got a great deal of satisfaction from doing a job that met his high standards.

My father's station wagon was always heavily loaded with upholstery samples that had to be piled up before one could get into the back seat, let alone sit there. But you know what? He knew where to grab the sample pack every time for a particular design or color a customer wanted. Talk about a filing system! Grandpa Eisman also had an old red truck that was used for hauling bigger furniture pieces and an old tarp that covered the furniture. George, the friendly part-time handyman at the shop occasionally assisted in the transporting of furniture.

In the city of Melrose Grandpa Eisman had good friends and was warmly accepted as one of the few Jewish businessmen in the area at the time. He had become a Mason in the 1970's and was quite proud of this accomplishment. Becoming a Mason involved studying and knowing Masonic history and tradition and rituals as well as being involved in community service.

Late One Afternoon: Injury to Grandpa Eisman

My father's store was on the main street and often people would stop by to check out fabrics and inquire about reupholstering. One afternoon in the 1950's as it was getting dark, a woman stopped in and asked to use the bathroom. My father said, "okay" and the next thing he knew, he was hit on the head and knocked out briefly. The "woman" turned out to be a man in disguise who robbed my father and took merchandise! The police later apprehended him. After that my father was not so willing to let strangers use his bathroom.

Grandpa Eisman had a small coin collection that probably was started, Don reminded me on my recent visit to him, from the change he found in the sofas he was reupholstering. After these finds, he began examining coins given him in change at restaurants or other places when making purchases. My brother Don has his coin collection.

Grandma Eisman's Skills: Seamstress and Draper— and Dancer Too in the 1930's

My mother was an excellent seamstress and draper. She had told me that as young as age 10, she learned to sew by hand and often while still in Russia, she was asked to show other school children how to sew. As a draper later in the U.S., her job was to examine the garment on a model and decide whether it needed a tuck here or adjustment there. She was later offered a job modeling. "I had a good shape when I was young", she'd say when she told about her modeling offer that would "teach me how to walk and swing my hips." But my father, then her fiancé, objected to what I guess appeared inappropriate at the time for his future wife. Grandma Eisman later told me she thought she "was too timid for modeling" and probably would not have taken the job. But my father's objection resolved the issue at once.

My mother also talked often about going to a big dance with friends where she was asked by a Spanish dance instructor to dance a waltz. She was single at the time, she'd add, and she "loved to dance." When she told the story, she always described the black taffeta, full skirted dress she wore and had made, with a big red rose at the hip; she was obviously very flattered that the instructor chose her as his partner for this dance, and she won a $5 gold piece for the dance.

Fashions and Bridge in the 1930's - 1940's

My parents were a good-looking couple. Both were tall and dressed well. My mother's hair was styled like actress Dorothy Lamour's, (she starred in musicals with Bob Hope) in pompadour style that was in vogue then. (Some of the 1940's look can be seen today.) My mother wore shoes and clothes that were fashionable, and she always smelled nice. In those days, wearing a girdle or corset was a must for many women. My mother, my Auntie Rose and most women of their age promoted corsets as helping one's posture and health and said they were comfortable as well! These were long corsets with "bones" (several thin strips of metal spaced around the tight girdle to hold "everything" in place). They later tried but never convinced me to wear one! I can't believe similar-type girdles are coming back!

Shoes—wedgies or platforms or whatever was fashionable at the time, my Auntie Rose was the first to have them. Her husband, my Uncle Joe, was a supervisor in a shoe factory in Lynn, and he brought home to his wife the finest up-to-date shoes. I remember especially the platform shoes dotted with colored rhinestones that were the rage after World War II. Uncle Joe was proud to see his wife wearing his beautiful shoes.

Those were the days when hard-working men who became skilled in craftsmanship were able to earn a decent living to support their families. Factory workers like my Uncle Joe could also expect steadily rising living standards and a reasonable degree of economic security. Today I don't think we encourage enough young men and women who may wish to learn and develop a trade, a skill or a craft. These occupations, these skills are so needed by our society. I respect the carpenter, the plumber, the car mechanic and others for their knowledge and skill to build or repair what many of us haven't a clue about.

My father, who my brother and I always called "Daddy," also dressed well and was fun to be with. He had a great sense of humor—but he was the authority figure in our family. He had the final word on many things.

My parents enjoyed card games. With other couples, they played poker almost every Saturday night either at our home or another couple's home and then served up a *nosh* (snack). My mother was also a skilled bridge player. She joined a bridge club wherever she lived—Dorchester, Malden and Minneapolis. Her concentration was intense and she was almost always a winner. So bridge and cards were important recreation for both my parents.

Smoking and Pollution—Not Much Public Awareness

Both my parents smoked when we were growing up. There were no anti-smoking campaigns and health alerts; at least I don't remember them. They gave up smoking in later years—first my father in the 1960's, and then he tried to get my mother to quit as well. Grandma Eisman quit smoking in the early 1970's. Shortly after my Auntie Rose quit smoking too.

So Don and I grew up with second-hand smoke in our home, as did some of my cousins. Smoking was very common in the 30's and 40's. What did we working class families know of the dangers? Movies depicted smokers in glamorous situations among wealth and fame. Pollution was in the air, chemicals in the ground, fossil fuel burning factories were all around us—as we went on with our daily lives.

Today's Energy Alternatives: From "Your Father's Oldsmobile" to Ethanol and Hydrogen

But America was booming after World War II. People had jobs and were buying homes—typically the one level home with the picture window! And cars—big cars were being bought by families. Why—that was every family's dream. And what of the gasoline needed to fill their tanks? No one asked where it came from, as far as I can remember. It was cheap and plentiful. I don't remember anyone questioning gasoline fumes polluting our air. I remember my nice Uncle Joe who owned a black Oldsmobile; my, he shined that automobile up and was so proud of it. And when time came to trade it in—well another black Oldsmobile replaced the old one.

Finally as global warming from these fossil fuels has hit home, we are at last embarking on energy alternatives. For almost four years, I have owned and operated an ethanol fuel car. My 2003 Chrysler vehicle, as many of you know, is called an E85 FFV (Flexible Fuel Vehicle) which means it can operate on clean renewable ethanol made from corn grown by farmers in our own country. And equally important, ethanol reduces our dependence on foreign oil! The FFV part of it means because it is a flexible fuel vehicle, you can, in a pinch, fill your car with regular gasoline as well.

And then there are hybrids that use batteries and thus need less gasoline—these types of vehicles have been a popular alternative. Other grains and wheat, sugars and even grasses are more possible alternatives to gasoline. And would you believe some are experimenting with vegetable oil (yes…vegetable oil leftover from those great tasting french fries at restaurants) as a form of fuel for our vehicles? Michael Noble of Minnesotans for an Energy Efficient Economy is committed to jumpstarting the manufacture of the world's first hybrid car, using batteries and ethanol.

Get on the bandwagon. Call or e-mail your two senators and your congress people and local leaders. Tell them you want ethanol, the clean renewable domestic energy that reduces pollution, helps develop local jobs and reduces our dependence on foreign oil. And tell gas stations to consider offering ethanol in addition to gasoline. Ethanol also costs less at the pump. The price of a new ethanol FFV vehicle is the same as non-ethanol cars. I am heartened. The next energy alternative will be the hydrogen cell car but that's a bit of a wait. At any rate, we have come a long way in realizing the desperate need to protect our environment. Let's hope the necessary action will at last take place to reduce global warming by conserving energy and using alternative fuels to run our vehicles.

Turkish Baths: In Russia and in America

On a lighter side and back to the 1940's, I remember Grandpa Sam Eisman found "Turkish baths" relaxing and he would occasionally go with male friends to these baths. I had completely forgotten about this until just a few days ago while Dad and I watched the movie "Day of the Jackal" about the attempted assassination of President Charles DeGaulle. The attempted assassin hides in a Turkish bath in Paris, of all places, to avoid detection by police—but alas he is caught. At any rate, from what I have read, men's bathhouses were popular in the old country, i.e., Russia, and one of the first communal institutions that Jewish men wanted in their new land was a Turkish bath. I don't know if my father enjoyed this in Russia. But I do remember when I was a young child he went every so often to the Turkish bath to sit and banter with friends in a steamy room—this was his way of relaxing. I was told as a child that heavy perspiring cleansed the pores and was good for you.

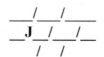

Chapter Seven
JUDAISM in our HOME:
FOOD SPEAKS the LANGUAGE

Preparing for the Holidays (1930's to 1955)

Jewish holidays in my parents' home meant the traditional holiday food would be prepared and served. At Purim, my mother baked *hamentashen* (triangular pockets of dough filled with prunes—ugh at the time) or poppy seed hamentashen. *Pesach* (Passover) was the time for *gefilte* fish, (*gefilte* means stuffed, you know), *knaedlach* (matzo balls), *farfel or matzo meal kugel or* the muffin-sized *kugela* (chopped or ground matzo with eggs and seasonings baked in muffin cups). This was a big holiday. Though we didn't search the house for *chometz* (leaven breads or bread products not permitted on Passover), my mother removed bread products and bagged and stored them in a special area. Tradition has it that you gather up all bread, cake and cookie products and bring them to a non-Jewish neighbor who burns the *chometz* for you. Or a family may bring their *chometz* to a non-Jewish family to enjoy—I like that.

My mother used a special set of dishes and silverware for the week of *Pesach*. The platters on which I serve our gefilte fish at Passover are the same ones my mother had served her gefilte fish for over fifty years. These platters were part of a set of dishes called "premium china" that were given to movie patrons in the 1940's! My mother had collected the entire set over a period of time and this was the *Pesach* set used in my parents' home in place of our everyday dishes. We had occasional family Seders with extended family, but mostly the food spoke the language of the holiday in our home. Much as my family loved bread, matzo was served and eaten for the entire week. It was only in recent years that I learned the "18 minute" matzo tradition. For Passover, when matzo is made from flour and water, it is carefully watched so that no water touches the flour prior to mixing for dough. It is then mixed and baked in less than eighteen minutes. The number "eighteen" you remember, means *Chai* (life). Foods that are *kosher* for Passover are baked under this same rabbinic supervision.

The holidays of Rosh Hashanah and Yom Kippur meant that after praying at *shul* (synagogue) and fasting on Yom Kippur, we would come home to break the fast, toast *l'chaim* (to life) and *Gott Yontiff* (Good Holiday) and sit down to Grandma Eisman's wonderful dinner. (Actually, the word "*yontiff*" is derived from the two Hebrew words *Yom* meaning day and *tov* meaning good.) The sweet finale at many holiday meals was the *Halavah* (crushed sesame seeds and honey), usually a mix of chocolate and vanilla. It was a treat—one little piece and your sugar fix was satisfied.

And finally the holiday of Chanukah which meant latkes, of course. My mother grated potatoes by hand (no food processors then) and cooked up the best latkes. She also made matzo meal latkes during Passover. (Recipes can be found in the Recipe Index.) When my *Zeyde* Eisman (my paternal grandfather) visited on occasion during Chanukah time in the 1940's, he would give us Chanukah *gelt* (money—pennies and dimes, sometimes quarters). That was special— or my *Bubbe* Kamsky would bring us Chanukah chocolate coins—like we have today—that hasn't changed! Although it's hard to believe, I don't remember a menorah in my parents' home when I was a child— that's the *emmes* (truth)—or do I remember getting Chanukah gifts from my parents. Occasionally at a relative's home, we lit the menorah. It's pretty amazing how my childhood Chanukahs compared with Chanukahs when you, my children (David, Pam and Joel) were kids— and more so, how Chanukahs of today that are a huge holiday. Obviously, Christmas has been a big factor in making Chanukah the big holiday that it has become.

Keeping Kosher or Not

My parents did not "keep a kosher home" which as you know means buying, cooking and eating food that meets rules of Jewish dietary law. Two separate sets of dishes and cooking utensils are required for the kosher home—one for meat and another for dairy. "Keeping kosher" also means the restriction of certain foods such as shellfish and pork. We did not drink milk with meat or chicken in my parents' home, although I don't think they would have objected—we preferred the ginger ale or coca cola. Nor did we eat pork or shellfish in our home; the exception was bacon that my mother often cooked "to warm our insides during winter," she'd say as she pressed out the fat onto paper bags. My brother Don and I ate fried clams at a nearby Howard Johnson's. I ate my first lobster in my teens when my friend Jeanette Klickstein Meltzer and I took a long weekend vacation to Cape Cod.

My mother did buy kosher meat and chicken, which she said, tasted better. Kosher beef and poultry, as many of you know, are slaughtered according to a ritual and approved by a *Mashgiakh* (Inspector of strict dietary observance). This ritual, which bothers me to write about it, is supposed to be quick and painless. I doubt it is. But I leave that to others to debate its worth in this regard. (Incidentally, did you know that Sweden requires animals be anesthetized before butchering?—now that's humane!)

Flicking Feathers off the Kosher Chicken in the 1930's and 1940's

When I was a kid up to around age 12 or 13, my mother would buy her chickens at a kosher butcher shop on Blue Hill Avenue in Dorchester. At the butcher shop, she and other shoppers purchased their often "still warm" chicken, stand at the counter and flick by hand the feathers off the chicken. Then the butcher would sear over a flame any remaining feathers left on the bird. At times I'd go with her, and I thought this must be what people everywhere did! I never thought it unusual at the time.

Then, of course, when you arrived home with your chicken, further "koshering" was required. To prepare a kosher chicken for cooking meant soaking it in cold water for one-half hour and then salting it with kosher salt to draw out any remaining blood followed by several rinses in cold water. Thus was your chicken ready for cooking.

Milchidak or *Flaishidik* (Dairy or Meat) and *Parveh* (Neutral Foods)

The word *pareve* or *parveh* means "neutral" food. For traditional Jews this neutral food is neither *milchidik* (dairy) nor *flaishidik* (meat) and so can be served with any type of food at any meal. So if you see the word *"parveh"* printed on a product, say a can of baked beans, this means that for those Jews who keep a kosher kitchen, this food is permitted with either dairy or meat.

The origin of separating meat from dairy has different versions. Biblical law mandates this and Orthodox Jews require it. Some Conservative Jews abide by the kosher rules as well. The moral explanation is that one should not drink the milk the mother feeds to her young and eat the meat of the mother during the same meal. Nor can a calf be cooked in a mother's milk. Biblical law states, "A mother and her young are forbidden to be slaughtered on the same day." In ancient times there may have been health reasons that stated milk and meat digest at an unequal rate and mixing these foods is difficult for the body to absorb. Today there is no health implication whatsoever regarding this. According to Lawrence Bush, author of several books on American Judaism, contemporary forms of kosher include "eco-kosher" which considers how crops are grown, harvested and packaged as important in deciding whether it is acceptable for use. Compassion for animals and the environment play a big role in today's Jewish baby boomers' lives.

As a child, I never even thought to ask about these rules. Since my parents did not keep a kosher home, this was not an issue for our immediate family. A number of my relatives did keep kosher homes. It is interesting that today at age 72, I am exploring these matters. It is never too late to learn and so I am finding some answers to questions I never asked as a child.

Chapter Eight
CELEBRATING the SABBATH
in our HOME

Preparing for *Shabbos* (Sabbath)

The Sabbath is the holiest day in Judaism; it is even more holy than Yom Kippur, which is something I did not know until recently. When Yom Kippur falls on a Saturday which it occasionally does, that would, of course, be the most holy day of all.

For centuries, after a long and often weary workweek, Shabbat—starting on Friday evening after sundown—was a most welcome break and meant for many Jews a time to relax and celebrate. It was a holiday every week. In years gone by, an old custom was for the father in the home to bless his children by placing his hand on their heads and recite a blessing. Isn't that nice? That is how rabbis now bless the Bar or Bat Mitzvah child.

Shabbat itself means "rest or cessation of labor." In many Jewish homes, a lot of preparation goes into getting ready for the Sabbath. In my parents' home, after the house was cleaned and dinner was cooked, my mother took her weekly bath, fixed her hair, creamed her face and put on clean clothes. Now she was ready to feed her family the Sabbath meal. The table was set for the occasion on a freshly pressed tablecloth awaiting food and family. Just before supper, my mother would *bentshen licht* (light candles) for *Shabbos* (with the accent on the first syllable—this is Yiddish). *Shabbat* (Hebrew) has the accent on the second syllable. The candles were usually lit at sundown or just before we all sat down for our meal. Why it wasn't a *family* ritual, I don't know. I suppose we just accepted what we were used to. When my *Bubbe* Kamsky lit the candles, she always first covered her head in respect for the Shabbat and then passed her palms over the candles, always towards herself. This was a practice that expressed that the soul is God's candle. The lighting of the Sabbath candles, one of the few *mitzvahs* (commandments or good deeds) that is even today usually reserved for Jewish women, and according to sources, makes her a "momentary" priestess.

The *Shabbos* (Sabbath) Dinner

The aroma of dinner was wonderful as we sat down to the traditional Sabbath meal of challah, roast chicken and chicken soup in that order. Why? Soup is filling and you might not leave room for the main course. This meal order was common in my extended family. Just before eating, of course, all through the 1940's and 1950's and beyond, came my parents' usual *l'chaim* (to life) and their *shnapps* (whiskey). If you remember, the *schnapps* in a shot glass was downed in seconds, usually followed by a chaser of seltzer—real bubbly soda water from a siphon. Even *Bubbe* Kamsky took her *schnapps* this way. In Dorchester, occasionally on weekends, my *Bubbe* would take the streetcar from nearby Roxbury where she lived to spend the weekend and share the *Shabbos* meal with us.

My *Bubbe* Kamsky at that time lived in an apartment on Warren Street in Roxbury. A dentist occupied the front section of the residence; a long hall separated the front section from the rear of the apartment. I didn't like the smell of the dental office so I would hurry to get to the back of the house where my *Bubbe* lived. *Bubbe* had a large bedroom, kitchen, and bathroom that were her living quarters. My favorite thing to do when I visited her as a child was to crank up or wind up her old RCA Victrola (phonograph player that played records—not an electric phonograph!) The Victrola was enclosed in a big and beautiful mahogany wood cabinet that was about as tall as I was at 10 years old in 1944. I'd maybe put on the 78 record of the Andrew Sisters (they were from Minnesota) who were "America's Wartime Sweethearts" singing "Under the Apple Tree" or the Yiddish *"Bei Mir Bist Du Shain"* (To Me You Are Beautiful) which my *Bubbe* enjoyed. My *Bubbe* Kamsky, fluent in Russian, never really learned to read and write English. Her name was the only English she could write. She understood spoken English well but usually responded mostly in Yiddish, sometimes asking at the end of her comments *"Farshtaist?"* (Do you understand?).

Myrna Kams Yunes, my cousin who is the daughter of Irving Kams (he shortened his last name when he went into music), also remembers the long walk back to *Bubbe's* living quarters. She and her two brothers hurried to see *Bubbe* who always welcomed them with a handful of M&M's. Myrna says *Bubbe* Kamsky kept the M&M's in a draw filled with mothballs so the candy taste was odd; still today they laugh at those memories.

When *Bubbe* Kamsky visited us, usually for the *Shabbos* weekend, she always brought for us a huge Hershey chocolate candy bar; even today when I see that size, I think of my *Bubbe's* visits and her Hershey bars. And my *Bubbe* knitted—socks, scarves and mittens seemed to just roll off her knitting needles in minutes. She donated a lot of her knitting to the Sinai Hospital in Boston. Once in a while on the weekend in the 1940's, we'd take a drive out "to the country," in the "machine" as my *Bubbe* referred to the automobile in those days—and I guess it was kind of like a machine. Some called the new automobiles "horseless carriages" when they first came out. Don't forget my *Bubbe* was born in 1878 so cars were a recent phenomenon for her. See photos of both my *Bubbes* in Photo Section.

Thus was the Sabbath celebrated in my parents' home. We typically did not go to *shul (synagogue)* but Friday night and Saturday were usually spent in a different more relaxed manner. My father was always home for the Saturday dinner around 2 p.m., taking his *dremel* (nap) on the "parlor" sofa (parlor passed down from the British), or if the sofa was in his shop waiting to be re-upholstered, he napped sitting on a stuffed parlor chair. He'd close his eyes and in minutes, he was asleep. If he drove back to his Melrose shop, it was for a short time.

In the Orthodox Jewish home and at the synagogue, Saturday was truly a day for praying and studying the *Torah,* which contains the first five books of the Hebrew Scriptures. In fact, under strict Jewish law, activities like writing, sewing, baking, driving and even answering the telephone are forbidden on the Sabbath. One's attention was to be on family, religion and study. Since my parents were not Orthodox, we did not abide by these rules, but I do remember that my mother would not sew on the Sabbath.

L'Chaim (To Life)!

Jewish families, especially at celebrations like the Sabbath and Passover have traditionally enjoyed wine, especially sweet wine. In my family, wine and liquor, preceded by the *l'chaim* toast was heard frequently and enjoyed in my parents' home and at family events, but *shikkers* (drunks) were unusual. Rarely do I remember hearing of a drunken relative or friend. If it did happen, someone might say it was *a shanda and a halb* (a shame and a half). Dancing at weddings, Bar Mitzvahs and other *simchas* (joyous occasions), you could hear someone call out it's *a lebedikeh velt* (a lively world) with *frailecha mentshen* (happy people)—often my mother said this. She so enjoyed these occasions. See my parents and siblings with their spouses at festive occasions in the Photo Section.

_/_ _/_
_/_ _/_S_
/   /

Chapter Nine
OBSERVING JEWISH HOLIDAYS
at the SYNAGOGUE

The High Holy Days

My parents did not typically attend Sabbath services. But they always went to services at Rosh Hashanah and Yom Kippur. Rosh Hashanah ushers in the Ten Days of Penitence when we look back at the year just past remembering the goodness or regrettably the not-so-good deeds we have committed. Yom Kippur is the time to atone for "one's sins," to ask for forgiveness from those we have hurt or been unkind to.

My parents always fasted on Yom Kippur when I was a kid. The Jewish Holidays for my friends and myself meant mostly dressing up and hanging around outside the *shul* (synagogue) looking for boys—while the older folks were inside "*davenen*" (praying). But I do remember my parents reminding us when the blowing of the Shofar (a ram's horn) would be heard. This sound signals the beginning of the ten-day High Holy Days—it takes skill and a lot of lung power to blow it and I liked hearing it. Today I like the tradition even more—the Shofar sound calls us all to peace and togetherness for a better and kinder world. At the closing of the Yom Kippur service, the Shofar is again sounded, concluding the ten-day High Holy days.

My father was the most committed to tradition going to *shul* regularly on the High Holy Days. When his mother died in 1947 he went to *shul* to say *kaddish* (mourner's prayer) almost every day for a full year. According to tradition, mourners say kaddish for one year until their loved one's soul is released from the body.

My mother always attended *Yiskor* services (service in commemoration of the dead) on Yom Kippur to pray for her father who had died, as I mentioned earlier, in 1934 just three weeks before I was born. The difference between *Kaddish* and *Yiskor* is that *Kaddish* is the prayer for the dead and *Yiskor* is the service for the dead.

Kaddish, the prayer for the dead is recited at Sabbath services, Rosh Hashanah, Yom Kippur and other Jewish holidays. In Orthodox Jewry, only those persons whose parent(s) were deceased recited the *Kaddish.* So as kids in an Orthodox synagogue, just before the *Kaddish* was to be recited, we young children—whose parents were still living—were asked to leave the sanctuary. Rabbi Sim Glaser of Temple Israel in Minneapolis tells me that traditional mourners, that is, Orthodox Jews, are only supposed to say *Kaddish* for children or spouses. Being sent out of the sanctuary perhaps was the custom in the particular *shul* that my parents attended. Today in Reform and Conservative Judaism all persons recite the *Kaddish* in memory of a departed friend or relative. As an adult, even though my parents were still living, I chose to recite *Kaddish,* in memory of deceased family or friends and those who perished in the Holocaust. However, when my parents were with me, I adhered to their tradition and would not say *kaddish.*

Lighting the *Yahrtzeit* Candle

In our family, Grandma and Grandpa Eisman always lit *yahrtzeit* (anniversary of one's death—or literally year's time) candles to commemorate the death of one of their parents, as do Dad and I today to commemorate the deaths of our parents. Dad and I light the *yahrtzeit* candle, which burns for 24 hours, and we say a little prayer remembering our parents. As you know, either the English or Hebrew calendar can be used for lighting *yahrtzeit* candles. For example, if you look at Temple Israel's Hakol (newsletter), both the English and Hebrew month and year are shown. As I write today on February 12, 2005, it is the month of Adar in the year 5765 that most Orthodox Jews believe dates back to Adam and Eve. The Hebrew calendar is a lunar calendar meaning the new month occurs with a new moon every 28 days. My parents always used the Hebrew calendar for their parents' *yahrtzeits* as do many Conservative and Orthodox Jews. Dad and I use the English calendar for remembering our parents' *yahrtzeits.*

A Little Distinction but a Big Difference: *Kaddish* vs. *Kiddish*

To flash forward a bit for the moment, around the time we were preparing for my grandson Sam's Bar Mitzvah, I remember Sue, my daughter-in-law asking the distinction between *KAddish* and *Kiddish* and we discussed this. It is confusing because only one letter "a" or "i" makes the difference. As explained above, *Kaddish is* the prayer for the dead. But *Kiddush* is the happy prayer over the wine and is recited on the Sabbath.

Hebrew Education and Bar Mitzvah: Reserved for Boys Only in the 1940's

After my brother Don was Bar Mitzvahed, he occasionally joined my father at services. In preparation for his Bar Mitzvah, Don attended *cheyder* (Hebrew school—the room or *shul* where Hebrew was taught) for a number of years. Mr. Yumans, his teacher was trained to instruct a number of boys on Hebrew pronunciation and Hebrew prayer. The language focused on Hebrew prayer especially prayers for the Sabbath and for the Bar Mitzvah. Hebrew was not taught as a living and speaking language as it is today in most Hebrew schools.

I did not learn Hebrew as a kid nor did I have any type of religious education. My paternal cousin Dorothy studied Hebrew, along with her two brothers, although she did not have a Bat Mitzvah because that was not permitted in Orthodox Judaism. My maternal cousin Myrna, born in 1948 so younger than my cohort, said she studied Hebrew for a short time but then she "became more interested in boys" and so dropped Hebrew study. None of my girlfriends studied Hebrew. Hebrew education and particularly Bar Mitzvahs at the time were a tradition in

Orthodox and Conservative Judaism and a celebration for boys only. It was at the age of 25 when Dad and I and little David moved to Kingston, New York in 1959 that I first studied and learned Hebrew. My teacher was the wife of our Reform Rabbi. That was a new and satisfying experience for me.

The Bat Mitzvah, as you know, began in Judaism's Reform Movement as a way of equalizing and sharing this celebration with girls as well as boys. Rabbi Sim Glaser of Temple Israel in Minneapolis tells me that the first Bat Mitzvah was held for Judith Kaplan Eisenstein in March 1922 when she was 12 years old.

Although Orthodox Jews still do not have a formal congregational Bat Mitzvah for girls, Rabbi Glaser tells me they do have a "sort of coming of age ceremony, sometimes called a Bas Torah where the young lady comes up to the bima to read something scriptural, but not from the Torah scroll itself."

Chapter Ten
THE PEARL HARBOR ATTACK: WORLD WAR II BEGINS

The Japanese Bomb Pearl Harbor

It was at my cousin Jerry's Bar Mitzvah weekend in December 1941, when I was seven years old, that we all heard on the radio that the Japanese had bombed Pearl Harbor! It was shocking news and we all huddled around the family radio to hear more. The next day President Roosevelt declared war on Japan followed right after by war declarations on Germany and Italy. World War II would change us forever. The war involved over 15 million American military and over 400,000 of them died. Another one million were wounded. It also cost the lives of 50 million military and civilians worldwide. It was a war fought to destroy Hitler, a monstrous dictator who wanted to exterminate all Jews, people with disabilities, Gypsies and homosexuals. Jews were hunted down, humiliated in public and then put in boxcars to be sent to their deaths in concentration camps. This inhumanity was as horrific as anything could ever be.

Hitler wanted to take over the world, starting with Europe and annihilate all the Jewish people in the process. The shadow on FDR's reputation was that, although he knew of the Holocaust, he did not move directly to interrupt the movement of Jewish prisoners to the death camps. Eleanor Roosevelt helped many Jewish individuals in Europe but she always felt she had not done enough, and thus later became an ardent supporter of Israel, according to political historian

Michael Beschloff who was on Public Radio today (March, 2005).

Although all wars are terrible, World War II was a necessary war—it needed to be fought to save the world from the dictator Hitler. I consider myself a pacifist, against wars, against violence, always in favor of diplomacy and negotiation. Still, whenever I hear the moving statement by Prime Minister Winston Churchill who vowed England would never give up its fight against the Nazis, I choke up. Here is some of what he said:

"…We shall fight on the seas and oceans; we shall fight…in the air, we shall defend our island, whatever the cost may be; we shall fight on the beaches, we shall fight on the landing grounds, we shall fight in the fields and in the streets, we shall fight in the hills; we shall never surrender."

War Bonds and Food Rations

In America meantime, people were quick and willing to help out with the war effort in any way we could. Women quickly took over jobs left unfilled by departing American servicemen. Food rations were issued for meat, butter, sugar, coffee and more; such foods were needed for our servicemen and women. My mother shopped carefully with our family ration books—often I was with her as she thought about what to buy with her weekly ration stamps. There were different colored stamps for different foods. Nylon stockings were hard to come by—I guess the nylon was needed for parachutes. Many families purchased government War Bonds when they could to help in the war effort. I remember our family purchasing war bonds for many years whenever my parents had the extra money. Citizens took up collections of aluminum and pots and pans since metals were needed to build ships and planes. Many homemakers collected grease from cooked foods—I can't remember why, but I do remember my mother collecting grease, storing it in tin cans and then bringing it somewhere. It was said later that most of these collections were never really used—the collection campaign was done to help Americans feel they were doing something useful during the war.

Grandpa Eisman, Air Raid Warden

There were periodic air raids when a siren would sound and

everyone had to hurry home, put out the lights and stay calm. This was to keep our skies darkened in case the U.S. was ever bombed. My father was a neighborhood air raid warden, which meant he wore a hardhat and carried a flashlight during these air raids checking to be sure lights were out in our neighborhood and people were safely in their homes. I remember being proud of him. A Russian immigrant, now an American citizen, he was happy to do his patriotic duty.

Everyone listened to the radio, read newspapers and watched the war unfold in the movie newsreels. World War II lasted six years (1939-1945) though as I mentioned, America did not declare war until Pearl Harbor was attacked in 1941. Patriotism in the United States was remarkable and intense. Kate Smith, heavy in appearance but strong in voice, moved everyone when she sang "God Bless America." This popular American favorite was heard often—in newscasts and on the radio. Still today when I hear Kate Smith's rendition, I fill with emotion.

The Diary of Anne Frank, the book the teenager had written while in hiding with her family in Holland for two years, became a worldwide favorite when it was found and published after the war. Sadly, Anne Frank died of typhus in a concentration camp.

Almost everyone knew of or had family members who were killed or injured in the war. Of course, as my grandkids know, Grandpa Ira, Grandpa Herb and Papa Gene served bravely in the military during World War II. If you are lucky to have grandparents still living who served in World War II, ask them sometime about their war experiences—they will probably have lots to tell you. My parents' family had cousins and friends who were in the army and in the navy; sadly Mrs. Kaplan, our next-door neighbor in Dorchester lost her son in the war. A blue star in a window signified someone in that family was serving in the war; a gold star sorrowfully told you a family member had been killed in the war. There were blue and gold stars everywhere.

World War II Ends

When Japan surrendered in 1945, World War II at last was over. Popular newscaster Tom Brokaw called the men and women who achieved victory in this battle "The Greatest Generation" and wrote a book of the same name. Most of you who remember the end of World War II probably remember the photograph taken in Times Square of a young sailor passionately kissing a nurse in sheer joy at our victory. That famous photo was taken by Jewish photographer Alfred Eisenstaedt and was seen by millions around the world.

In the years before and after World War II, Australia proved to be a great sanctuary for Jews. In the 1930's, seven thousand Jewish refugees from Germany and Austria found haven in Australia. Following the war, tens of thousands of Holocaust survivors were admitted into the country. I did not know this at the time, but I recently read about it in World Jewish Congress literature. Today Australia has the highest percentage of Holocaust survivors of any Jewish community in the world.

The Success of the GI Bill

After the war ended, the GI Bill was introduced and passed in Congress. This new legislation provided World War II veterans the opportunity to get a college or vocational education paid for by the government for their sacrifices in the war effort. GI's flooded college campuses and this, in turn, helped the country's labor market. Why? Unemployment would have been huge with all the returning veterans. But it was reduced because many veterans were in colleges and vocational schools and this, in turn, helped to train and educate them for better paying jobs that awaited them upon their completion of their education. They could look forward to a higher standard of living for themselves and their families.

The GI Bill also provided low interest home and farm mortgages so that veterans could purchase a home or farm for themselves and their families. My grandkids know their Grandpas Ira and Herb and their Papa Gene took advantage of these GI benefits, either to go to college or to buy their first family home. The nation was mighty grateful for the sacrifices made by our World War II veterans, and in establishing the GI Bill, started an economic surge in our country that benefited millions of Americans.

President Roosevelt's Pretense: Hiding His Disability

FDR was one of the most popular presidents of our time. During the depression, he helped to create jobs that put people back to work and he succeeded in getting America going again. He was a close ally of Winston Churchill and together, with other allies and with the brave men and women who fought and those who sacrificed their lives, Hitler and Nazism were defeated and World War II ended. During his twelve years as President, FDR's wife, Eleanor worked actively for all Americans, particularly the poor and the sick and traveled around the country to see which of FDR's programs were working or wasteful or under funded. If there was ever a Co-President, Eleanor Roosevelt was that person. (Shortly thereafter Congress passed legislation limiting a president's term to two or a total of eight years in the White House).

While many Americans knew President Roosevelt had polio, many did not know that he was unable to walk without assistance. Attitudes towards people with disabilities at the time were unkind and the President and the administration feared people would think the President weak. FDR was never photographed in a wheel chair and his black braces were covered by trousers longer than usual. The media that reported on the President would not discuss that FDR's legs were paralyzed for fear of public disapproval and damaging FDR's image. Only much later was President Roosevelt's condition fully revealed to the public. Today I am sure such a cover-up would not occur. We are hopefully a nation that values political leaders, as well as others, for their leadership, their vision and their caring. One's disability, I believe, should never be a factor in one's ability to lead. President Roosevelt died of a stroke in April 1945 just weeks before the war ended. The nation and the world mourned his death.

_____/ I /_____
___/_____/___
___/_____/

My Maternal
Bubbe
Breina
Kamsky
circa 1920s

News from Chernigov

IRVING
KAMSKY
Bar Mitzvah
1922-3
in Boston

Bubbe Kamsky
holding
Sylvia Kamsky
1905

NOMI KAMSKY
in Russia
1928
(Nomi was
brother of
Sylvia & Rose
Nomi did not
come to US)

Auntie Rose Kamsky
My Bubbe Breina Kamsky
Uncle Irving Kamsky
My Mother Sylvia Kamsky
My Zeyde Harry Kamsky
The Kamsky Family
circa mid 1920's
in America.
Brothers
Schnaer &
Nomi & Nomi's
wife Marusi
circa 1925
in Russia
Breina Kamsky
& children
Standing L to R
Daddle, Sylvia
Seated L to R
Rose, Irving
circa 1915
in Chernigov
Russia
Nomi Kamsky
& mandolin
circa:
early 1900's
He was a
musician.
Manifest of Kamsky Passengers Debarking from
the ship "Berengaria" at Ellis Island N.Y. 1922
My Bubbe & Zeyde Kamsky
circa late 1920's
Boston

My Father Sam Eisman   My great grandfather Dvecah   Koppel   Aunt Nolly   My Bubbe Frieda Eisman   Uncle Izzy Eisman

Вы говорите по-английски?
(Do you speak English?)

Он говорит по-русски.
(He speaks Russian.)

Откройте двери!
(Open the door!)

A Bit of Russian Language

The Eisman Family in Russia circa 1911

Ely Lerman and new wife Becky Eisman Lerman in America circa 193?

My paternal grandfather Frank Eisman and daughter Becky circa 191?

SYLVIA & SAM EISMAN'S Wedding   May 1931

Sam on bended knee
proposing to Sylvia
1930

HONEYMOONING 1931

Sylvia. Donny + Harriet Eisman +
Mrs. Lilly + Earl. Marilyn + Ralph. 1942

"Daddy's
Famous
John Hancock"
1938

Sam + Sylvia Eisman and
son Donny 1933

Sisters Rose Winthrop, Sylvia Eisman
with children. L to R: Donny, Walter
Harriet + Jerry. Joe Winthrop in back
1937

Sam Eisman + Kids
Donny + Harriet 1935

Donny + Harriet
crashing Donny
of Greenock st
Dorchester 1939

Jerry Winthrop, Donny + Harriet
circa 1937

Sam Eisman geb work with WPA in
the DEPRESSION. 1938

World War Two

Don Eisman's BarMitzvah 1946

Harriet Eisman
1946

L to R: Sam, Sylvia, Don and Harriet
at Don Eisman's BarMitzvah

Millie & Izzy
Eisman and
Kids Florence
& Charlotte
1946

Sam & Sylvia
Eisman
1946

From Sylvia Eisman's Recipe Book

Brownies

1/4 lb. of butter
2 cups of sugar
4 eggs
3 kg of bak chocolate
2 teaspoons of vanila
1 1/2 cups of flour
1/2 cup . . . milk
1 . . . . . . nuts
cream butter and
sugar then add
everything
. . . . in 350 degrees
for 45 minutes

L to R: Walter Winthrop, Sylvia Eisman, Jeanette Winthrop circa 1950's

BLINTZES

Taiglach

Cold Shav

Matzo Ball Soup

GRIBBENES

My mother used to make gribbenes; David especially loved it as a chi . . . it's unhealthy because it is loaded with chicken fat—but I include . . . posterity and for . . . occasional nosh.

This recipe renders *schmaltz* (chi . . . some of the chicken skins and . . . and onions are mighty tasty . . . stored for cooking, e.g., . . . sautéed for chopped liv . . . the simple recipe.

Gefilte Fish

Remove fat from chicken and . . .
Cook fatty pieces and skins over . . . because fat . . .
splatter. After a few minutes, add one large . . . chopped onion and stir until fat . . . onion pieces are crisp and brown. Drain on paper towels. Pass around as a *nosh* (snack . . . with challah or other bread. Can also be used as topping on baked potato.

EISMAN FAMILY HOME 1949-1901 35 HAWTHORNE ST. MALDEN, MA

My Maternal Bubbe Braina Kanofsky Circa 1950's

My Paternal Bubbe Frieda Eisman circa 1940's

Relatives Visit. Hawthorne St. Malden circa 1950's

COUSIN Dorothy Margolis 1953

circa 1950's SAM and SYLVIA EISMAN

pe Of The Year: Stage Door ~ 1951

By Edna Ferber and George S. Kaufman

Harriet Eisman 1951
Malden High School Graduation

ARTHUR MoYNADZIAN 1951

Marilyn Savage + Harriet 1951

Harriet Eisman High School Grad and Agron Levine Boyfriend, 1951

Don Eisman 1951

Harriet + Sandra Radman 1951

Harriet + Parents, Sam + Sylvia and Don

1951

College Friends at Boston University
Elaine Naanis 1955
Wilma Zinman 1951

Rose Krichstein 1955

Ira and Harriet Pointing... friends Jeanette Meltzer (in white hat) Elaine Naanis and Wilma Benjamin 1955

Just Engaged! Ira (looks dazed) and his parents, Dora and Phil Reiss 1955

IRA + HARRIET 1955

Friends Arlene and Mel Kahn 1958

Dan back from Germany for wedding 1955

work Friends 1955

Florence, Charlotte + Aunt Millie Eisman, Aunt Molly + Dorothy – 1955

TWO HAPPY FATHERS
Phil Reiss + Sam Eisman 1955

Ira and Harriet's Wedding 1955

L to R: Don, Bubbe Kamsky, Ira, Harriet, Sylvia + Sam Eisman

L to R: Phil + Dora Reiss, Ira, Harriet, Carol

Cousins and Friends 1955

Eisman Relatives 1955

Chapter Eleven
MORE FAMILY MEMORIES

Jitterbugging to the Big Bands in the 1940's

At happier times, my cousin Walter and I would jitterbug to swing music on the sun porch of his parents' home—that was fun. He was my first dance partner! And my "kissin' cousin." My memories of those days are as vivid as if they had happened yesterday. When my brother Don and I were kids, our parents and my Auntie Rose and Uncle Joe and my cousins exchanged overnight visits at each other's homes when they lived in Methuen and then in Lawrence, MA—towns north of Boston and almost two hours away from Dorchester where we lived until 1949. When Jerry Winthrop was in law school in Boston, he sometimes came to our house for supper. I remember his pacing the kitchen floor, hands in pockets, asking how everything was. My mother liked it when he once commented "Auntie Sylvia has nice legs." My mother repeated this often during the years ahead.

The relationship between the two sisters—my mother and my Auntie Rose—wasn't always so rosy. There were occasional rifts, as happens in many families. One in particular broke the family apart for months when I was about 13 or 14 years old. I cannot remember the particulars but I was asked by, I think my father, to go to my Auntie Rose's home to help mediate the problem. So off I went on a bus to do the job of family negotiating. I don't recall what was said or discussed but I do remember the meeting was successful and the rift was healed.

My mother's brother, Irving Kams became a high school music teacher and played the saxophone and clarinet for big time bands. Always fun to be with, my Uncle Irving sometimes entertained us playing his sax. Sadly, he died of brain cancer in 1978. His wife is Jeanette and she lives near her three children in the Boston area.

When I asked for family memories, Harold Kams, Myrna's older brother wrote a sweet e-mail remembering a visit he and his family took to my parents' home when he was about 13. After cooking and serving up chicken for the company, my mother found, Harold says, that there was not much left for her. "I love to eat the bones and around the bones. The best parts of the chicken are the bones," Harold writes, she had said. And he says he remembers this whenever he serves chicken. He grabs for the bones!

Hanging Out with My Cousins

On my father's side, my cousin Dorothy and I shared growing-up stories. I remember tweezing her eyebrows on one of her visits to our house. She is two years younger than I so she was the recipient of some of my clothes that my mother had sewn. Who could know that years down the road she would be the family's most successful business woman, owning her own company and driving her Mercedes Benz! And my cousin Murray, her brother? Why, he was the electronic expert in the family who, in the 1960's with a team of others talked of scanning items into a data system that would eventually become the Bar Code System.

When I was about 13, it was time to send the old piano that I had played and taken lessons on to Cousin Dorothy. So it was moved from our second story flat to her home on Creston Street in Roxbury. I remember it being lowered from our front porch onto the street with rope—maybe it was too big to be carried down the stairs. My mother said I became more interested in boys and records than piano.

Buying records in those days was fun. To listen to a record you might want to buy, you'd take the record into a soundproof room and play it. My friend Ruthie bought a lot of records; I mostly listened. On a 78 record, only one song was heard on each side. These records could break easily so you had to be real careful in handling them.

My Cousin Dorothy's sweet and giving mother, my Auntie Molly, was proud of her three kids; she was basically the provider for her family and the nurturer as well. But Dorothy's father, my Uncle Max always greeted us warmly whenever we saw him. My father called my Auntie Molly the peacemaker and my mother said she was a *gotte neshome* (good soul) because she was always helping others despite her own problems and her family's meager means. My cousins Florence and Charlotte Eisman, daughters of my Uncle Izzy and Auntie Millie lived in nearby Roxbury and we visited together on some occasions.

Life in the 1940's and 1950's had a gentler touch, it seemed. Granted, there was a lot more prejudice and discrimination against minorities and women, so the simplicity of those years in many ways maybe was a cover for the underlying inequality that existed. Inequality, social justice and lack of national health care remain challenges in our country, but citizens are far better off today than half a century ago. At least today most discrimination is illegal.

My Auntie Becky (sister of my father) and Uncle Ely Lerman lived in Lynn and had a huge furniture store in that city. They were wealthy but not too generous with their wealth. I remember my Uncle Ely's greetings. First the hug, then the big pinch on my left cheek. Once I surprised him with a big sourball candy in my left cheek. "Pretty clever," he said, laughing. I liked my Uncle Ely's easy smile. The Lermans did not have children. It was said that my Auntie Becky brought home an infant, maybe from an adoption agency with the intention of adopting the child, but when the infant cried most of the night, the next day Auntie Becky returned the child to the agency.

Memories of my girlhood are family centered. Visiting with relatives was always fun and the adults took great pride in their children's accomplishments, expressing their pleasures often in Yiddish. If asked, even in recent years, the literal translation of a particular Yiddishism, sometimes I was and still am unable to give it. But I know and feel the emotions surrounding the expression. Here's a popular Yiddishism that's often confusing. A Jewish grandmother might answer that her grandchildren are wonderful *kineahora* (thank God—we are so blessed). But the expression *Git mir nisht kayn eynhoreh* (don't give me the evil eye) was uttered to ward off bad fortune or predict bad outcomes. So, as you see the Yiddish sounds are similar, but their meanings are hugely different.

Our Canadian Cousins

My father's Canadian cousins were the Appotive family, and they were important and close to my father and the rest of us. Uncle Avraham (my paternal grandmother's brother) and Auntie Surah helped raise my father and his siblings in Russia after his father left for America to find work in preparation for bringing the rest of the family to America. The Appotives later settled in Ottawa and Montreal and we visited back and forth whenever we could. There were four brothers in their family (Rudy, Joe, David and Benny) who were my father's cousins and we tried to share in each other's *simchas* (joyous occasions) whenever we could. David's daughter, Sharon Appotive and Rudy's daughter-in-law, Carolyn Appotive have recently completed a beautiful and extensive history of the Appotive family, complete with pictures and other memorabilia.

The Hospital on Harvard Street

In Dorchester in the 1940's we lived just a few houses away from the Boston State Mental Hospital where, in the section near our street, the female patients resided. The entire facility was enclosed in a black iron fence. We were just kids—my friends and I—but curious as well, so we'd stop to talk to the women behind the iron-gated fence. Most were young; some seem confused; others were friendly. Many wandered aimlessly around the grounds of the hospital. Basically, the hospital was custodial in nature, I guess—that is, I doubt if there was much in the way of treatment for these troubled and distressed residents. It was no big deal, that is, no worry living so close to such a hospital. When I think back to those days, it's sad to think of those young women "locked up"—I wonder what kind of therapy, if any, they received and what happened to many of them.

Anti-Semitism in Boston: Our Experiences

I talked earlier of the anti-Semitic attacks my parents endured in Russia. Grandma Eisman's 16-year-old brother, Dobby and my paternal great-grandmother Dvorah were both killed during the pogroms perpetrated by anti-Semitic hoodlums. Coming to America hopefully meant my parents and their families could live freely as Jews.

For sure, there was anti-Semitism in Boston but we did not experience it living in the mostly Jewish neighborhood of Dorchester. Neither Don nor I can recall any overt anti-Semitism towards our parents or us. That was during the 1930's and 1940's. In 1949 when I was 15 we moved to Malden where my classmates were mostly non-Jewish and Don continued as a student at the prestigious Boston Latin School where he recalls good relationships among the mostly Irish students. Many of my good friends in Malden were not Jewish. Religion never seemed an issue. Even my father whose business was located in Melrose, MA, a mostly Christian community, was accepted and welcomed by the city's business people and community leaders.

My cousin Walter lived with his family in Methuen, MA, just north of Boston for a few years before moving to Lawrence, MA. There he did run into a kid who used anti-Semitic slurs. Walter punched him in the face, bloodying his nose. My Uncle Joe told Walter that was a good response. This kid never said anything to Walter again.

Maybe we were lucky. Of course we know anti-Semitism is still present in many parts of the country; and in Europe, there is grave concern about its spread. Here in Minnesota we live in a diverse and accepting community. This was not the case in the 1930's through the 1950's. Back then, with the exception of St. Mary's Hospital, Jewish doctors were not allowed to practice in local hospitals in Minneapolis. And so Mt. Sinai hospital, now closed, was built to accommodate Jewish physicians and their patients. Hard to believe, isn't it? Edina, in particular, would not sell or rent homes to Jewish people. Thankfully, the situation began to change in the 1960's, and today the Twin Cities is one of the most diverse and integrated and accepting communities in the country. However, we must be forever vigilant and support religious freedom for all.

___/_C__/___
___/___/___
  /   /

Chapter Twelve
SCHOOL DAYS and BEYOND

Elementary School Years

I liked school as a kid at the Robert Treat Paine Elementary School in Dorchester. After about six weeks in 1st grade, my teacher and the school principal recommended that I be moved up to 2nd grade—a "double promotion," they called it. The teacher and principal thought I could read and write at a higher level and was emotionally prepared for such a move. My parents at first questioned this idea but then were delighted. My mother bragged about my "double promotion" when I first met Dad! I had just turned 17 when I graduated from high school in 1951.

When I was maybe about 10, I helped out after school at a small nursery school in a private home behind my elementary school. It was a voluntary thing—I did not get paid. I don't know how I came upon that but I know I always liked little kids. (Strange this should come to me—but years later at this private home, a young woman climbed out of the second story window and stood on the roof, threatening to jump (she was not the nursery school teacher!). I can't remember if she jumped or not. I don't think she did.

At my elementary school I was taller and looked older than most girls my age. In the early 1940's a child's movie ticket cost, if I remember correctly, 25c or less. You had to be 12 or younger, and I'd often have to show my birth certificate as proof of my age. I think I was in a hurry to grow up because I always told my mother to tell boys I was older than I really was. Bobby socks and saddle shoes—later penny loafers—were in fashion. My family skimped when buying clothing but then my mother made most of my clothes and hers too.

Good quality shoes, however, were a must to protect growing feet, so before each school year off we'd go to Braverman's on Blue Hill Avenue for new shoes. (The memory of Mrs. Braverman, her graying hair neatly pulled back, bringing out shoeboxes is as vivid for me today as though it happened yesterday.) Pants in those days were worn only for warmth; otherwise we wore skirts, usually with blouse and cardigan sweater. Pin curls (small curls twirled on your finger and held in place with bobby pins)—that was the ritual before bedtime if you wanted your hair to "look nice" the next morning. Imagine sleeping with that in your hair? Yet I did this probably two or three time a week.

In those days, knickers for boys were popular. Knickers were pants gathered loosely, then banded with elasticized trim just below the knee. I don't ever remember my brother Don objecting to wearing them—all young boys wore them. Dad tells me he remembers moving "up" from knickers to regular pants in 1938 when he entered 8th grade.

"Lassie Come Home!"

My favorite movies were the "Lassie" features. I loved that big collie. I almost always cried when Lassie was found and reunited with her little pal. I read recently that although Lassie was female in the movies, six different collies, all MALE, played the role all through the years. Female dogs shed when in heat, so the story goes—so only males were used and the dog's anatomy carefully disguised. The "Lassie" story later became a television show, winning Emmys for the "Best Kids' Show" in the early 1950's. Today there are people from that era still collecting "Lassie" memorabilia.

Affection Plentiful in the Eisman and Kamsky Households

Although I've mentioned the discipline that was expected in my parents' home, there also was a lot of physical affection expressed in our family and extended family, especially among the women. I remember my *Bubbe* Kamsky's big wet kisses against my cheek. No one was really shy about touching and hugging.

I want to tell you an amusing and naïve childhood story. From the time I can remember, whenever my mother hugged me, I noticed the small light-colored round birthmark about the size of a pea in the center of her chest. It was cute—it looked like it was deliberately planted there. And so I thought this was what all grown-up women had—a small birthmark right in the middle of their chests! I guess I never asked—it was way later that I figured it was my mother's special birthmark. And until her last days, every time I saw the birthmark, I remembered my childhood feelings about it.

In addition to frequent hugging in the Kamsky and Eisman families, there was praise too—often expressed in Yiddish. *Oy, a mazel em in kop* (Oh, good health or good luck to your head or you have a good and kind head) was heard often when one of us did something thoughtful for another person. Grandma Eisman would say this frequently to my kids when they were little. When a smart person gives information he is the *chochum* (wise man)—both syllables pronounced like Ch in Challah. Grandpa Eisman laughingly would say my young son was a *chochum,* when he "gave advice" to his younger siblings. Likewise, empathy or support was given, usually in Yiddish. If a family member was feeling sad about an event, the advice from my mother or my Auntie Rose might be *a deigeh nisht* (forget about it or don't worry, said with understanding). If you were troubled about something, my mother would say *fradranesht deine kop* (don't worry about it—literally, don't mix up your head). These bits of advice weren't exactly what a therapist might say—but they were intended to make a person feel better and they usually worked.

When my Auntie Rose had an idea to tell us, she would start her statement with *Chesach Chein (*Listen up or be attentive). My spelling may be off here; this was her expression to get our attention to something she wanted us to hear. I smile to myself as I write this and picture my Auntie Rose speaking to us. And we did listen up. Another Yiddish expression I heard often from my father, was *Efsher* (maybe, could be)—it was actually Dad who reminded me recently of this expression. I haven't really heard Yiddish spoken since my mother died in February 2001. I am glad I'm finishing up this book before I forget all my Yiddish.

_E_ /___/____
___/___/____
/   /

Chapter Thirteen
A MIX of MEMORIES: SOME SAD

Personal Heartbreak and Poignancy in the mid 1930's

Raising children, cooking and keeping house brought my mother great happiness. But in later years, she told me about a very sad event that had occurred around 1935 in her life. My brother was just over two years old and I was about ten months old in 1935 when my mother found that she was pregnant for the third time. I guess my parents had been told and believed if a woman was breast-feeding, she could not get pregnant. (Although pregnancy is more difficult while breast-feeding, it is not impossible.) It was still the depression and money was scarce. How would my parents manage yet another baby in these difficult times?

Abortions were illegal at that time—who would they turn to for help? My father's older cousin intervened. She felt their economic situation required they take steps to terminate this pregnancy, and I guess they agreed with her. So this cousin (who shall remain unnamed) sent my mother to a pharmacist who concocted a rather toxic brew that my mother drank. She became very ill but did not miscarry. So my mother was sent to yet another "doctor" who did some type of procedure which caused her to hemorrhage profusely, and she was rushed to the hospital.

Finally, with emergency medical attention, the bleeding stopped and she began to recover. The pregnancy had been terminated. This is indeed a lesson that abortions should remain safe and legal. My mother was asked over and over while in the hospital to name the doctor who had done the procedure that caused her to miscarry and hemorrhage, but she refused to reveal his name. When the hospital administrator came in to see her, she told me the nurse said, "This is the lady who won't talk." A sad story especially because my mother loved children; at another more secure economic time, a third pregnancy would have been welcomed.

My Father's Illness: Tuberculosis

When my father was in his mid to late twenties, he became ill, lost weight and was hospitalized with tuberculosis. Luckily he was treated quickly and sent to a sanitarium to recover. My mother recalls his quick recovery and rapid weight gain from "eating bananas," she used to say. At any rate, because TB is so contagious, for many years after his recovery and during all my elementary school years, I was frequently called into the nurse's office to answer questions and be checked for my health. I was always embarrassed when the nurse entered the classroom, called out my name and asked me to come to her office. I was sure glad when these nurse requests ended.

Going to the Beach: A Close Call

Living near the Atlantic Ocean, summers in the 1930's and 1940's were spent going to the beach. Often my mother took us on a streetcar to Carson Beach to play in the sand and water. We never had swimming lessons as kids so I grew up a non-swimmer. I remember as a carefree child of eight or nine sitting in a tube floating along with the waves in the ocean when the tube slipped out from under me and I discovered I was over my head. I yelled and cried and splashed until a nearby man heard me and brought me to safety. After that, I began treating deep water as a bit treacherous, and I guess I have never fully recovered from my fear. It was only when David and Pam had swimming lessons in Iowa City that Dad and I also took lessons. It was the first—and I think the last—time I ever jumped off the diving board!

Pleasant Memories: *Vos Machstu?* (How are you?)

The streetcar was our public transportation everywhere growing up in Boston in the 1930's and 1940's. I rode it to junior high and high school—there were no school buses that I remember. If you lived near enough to school as I did in elementary school, you walked; otherwise you took a streetcar to school. So it was to the streetcar stop we went for our trip to Carson Beach in Boston. At the beach my mother would meet a friend or relative. The conversation, if in Yiddish, would go something like this: *Vos machstu?* (How are you?) *Vos hert zich?* (What's new?). If they had talked about a mutual friend's problems, I would hear something like she's *zayre farbissen* (very bitter) or *Er zitst oyf shpilkes* (He's restless; literally, he sits on pins and needles). Something might be *zayre gerfelech (very bad)* and meant *tsores* (trouble) for the entire family. It was nice to hear good things like she is a *gotte neshoma* (good soul) or *ich bein zayre tsifreden* (I am very happy or satisfied). And so on went the conversation until *zeit gezunt* (goodbye—literally be well). Then came time for the dip in the Atlantic Ocean for my Ma—*"oy a mekhaye"* (oh, a pleasure), she'd say at the refreshing feeling of the cold water on her hot body.

Get Out of the Wet Bathing Suit into Dry Clothes Ritual

At the beach we often ate egg salad sandwiches for lunch that my mother had prepared—they were good and, of course, we had our milk in an old thermos that did the job. If we were lucky later that afternoon, my mother gave us money to buy a cold bottle of tonic (coke or orange drink) that we all shared. (Fast-forwarding to our summer trip in 2002, you know "pop" is still called "tonic" in Boston.) If we got bad sunburns at the beach, vinegar was applied to cool your skin—it was cold and felt good. We did have "suntan lotion"—I don't think it provided much protection from the sun.

Anyway, when we were little (under about 8, I would guess), before packing up our stuff for the trip back home, we had a "get out of our wet suits into dry clothes ritual." My mother would wrap a towel around me (I always looked around anxiously to be sure no one was watching).

Then off went the wet bathing suit and on went the dry clothes followed by the sandy feet wash while sitting on a bench. Then it was Don's turn. (I don't remember what my mother did about her own wet bathing suit!) So with our dry *tushies* (behinds) and our clean feet, off we went to the streetcar.

Wearing clean, well fitting clothes was important. No *shlumpers* (untidy persons, careless dressers) in our home. You only need a little *saichel* (common sense) to know that clean, tidy clothing was a must.

Later Revere Beach, just north of Boston, became our summer escape. Don and I made friends with neighborhood kids. We'd play beach ball and bury each other in sand, leaving only one's head showing. And always a portable radio played the baseball game. The Boston Red Sox were huge in the 1940's and Ted Williams was everyone's hero. Hooray for the Red Sox winning the World Series in 2004.

Occasionally on weekends we drove to the beach with my father in his old station wagon, and as I mentioned earlier, it was always filled with upholstery samples so finding a place to sit was a trick—no seatbelts then—you sat wherever you found space. "You can smell the ocean," my father would say with pleasure as we approached the Atlantic Ocean. Car windows were wide open (no car air-conditioning then; at least we didn't have it), and the wind in our faces felt nice. At the end of the day at the beach my father summed up our experience, "Well, that's the whole story in a nutshell," something he often said after an event, usually pleasant, had come to its end.

When my father's business was beginning to prosper, my parents took us for a month's stay in one big room at an old hotel on Revere Beach, just north of Boston. There my mother cooked dinner in a hot (no air-conditioning) big room but was happy to look out the window to the vast Atlantic Ocean. The sea provided a breeze, my parents used to say—but I remember some very hot nights.

In the summer of 1948 we rented the upstairs of a house in Nantasket Beach, on the south shore of Boston. This was a step up from Revere Beach. I was 14 at the time and Don 16. I remember telling older boys I was 15 or 16—I looked older than 14, and most boys believed me.

Another family outing site was the Blue Hills, south of Boston, where we went for picnics. This huge recreation site had a bluish hue on the slopes when seen from a distance. Today the Blue Hills is a big ski resort. Nathan Farms was another day-vacation spot. Good meals were served in a farmhouse and there were lots of trees and open space. My parents really enjoyed the food and farm-like setting of Nathan's.

More Childhood Stories

We didn't have pets when I was a kid but one day we found a small injured bird (I think it was a wren) on our back porch. My mother laid a soft blanket in a box and gently placed the bird in it. Then she crushed hard bread into crumbs and put the dish with the crumbs and a bowl of water in the box. After a number of days the bird began flying around the porch and eventually flew away. It was a tender event and I remember it well.

Once when my brother and I were maybe under eight or nine and home from school with—I think—mumps, my mother decided we needed a walk and some fresh air. So off we went down Harvard Street passing the barking and unleashed German shepherd at the corner house. "Just keep walking...don't look at him!" was my mother's warning to us. I was always afraid he'd chase after us and bite me.

Outside we roller-skated, jumped rope, played hopscotch and rode bikes. Hide and Go Seek was popular then as it is now. After counting to 20, I remember the seeker would yell out "Alle Alle Entry" meaning, I guess, "All ye, All ye...come in," probably originally a British expression. Indoors we played school (I was usually the teacher); monopoly was a favorite game for Don and me. He usually won over me.

Sidewalks in the Neighborhood and my Friend Tibe

There were always sidewalks when I was a kid—that's where we roller-skated (the streets in Dorchester were cobblestone as were many streets in Boston at the time so impossible to skate on). It's sad so much of suburbia is without sidewalks. Sure, there is extra snow shoveling with sidewalks—even maybe more grass to cut. We had sidewalks in Iowa City when my three children were little. They learned to ride their trikes and bikes on safe sidewalks, and walkers appreciated sidewalk protection when pushing baby carriages. To save city or county tax funds by eliminating safe and fun sidewalks is a mistake, I think. There were no garages in our Dorchester neighborhood. Most people did not own cars; if they did, cars were parked on the street.

Anyway, when I was kid, roller skates were a kind of metal plate with 4 wheels that you slid your saddle shoes into and could be adjusted in length or width and tightened with a key; then the key on a shoestring went around your neck. I shared a two-wheeler boy's bike with my brother, but mostly my friend Tibe and I rented bikes for 25c an hour and biked to Howard Johnson's for ice cream cones.

One day when we were maybe under 12 years old, Tibe and I walked through nearby Franklin Field on Blue Hill Avenue to see what was going on. There might be a tennis game or a baseball game. We decided to stop and sit on a park bench. Suddenly a middle-aged man appeared before us, opened his raincoat and exhibited himself. Stunned—and very embarrassed and a little scared, we hurried home.

My friend Tibe was a pretty brave kid. As a little girl, she contracted polio (called Infantile Paralysis then), the same disease that President Roosevelt had that I discussed in Chapter Ten. Tibe wore a leg brace for a while but then after that came off, she jumped and ran and biked and played. Polio is a virus and in those days, there was no vaccine. So if this virus affected your central nervous system, it could cause paralysis as it did in FDR's legs. Many people had the disease but for most, symptoms were flu-like and were gone in days or weeks. Luckily, in the 1950's the Salk vaccine was developed and since then, polio vaccines have been further perfected. The March of Dimes was established by FDR to raise money and awareness about polio. Today polio is pretty much eradicated in the United States and the vaccine is helping to wipe out polio in the few nations that still have polio cases.

In addition to the sidewalks that I miss in suburbia, I remember fondly the front porches at most homes—porches where families and neighbors met and chatted. As I write, I remember my mother telling us that when we were toddlers, my brother tossed a small truck (metal, no plastics then) over the porch from our second floor flat that narrowly missed a walker below! Then my parents attached chicken wire around the three sides of the porch to prevent any future accidents. I like porches because they allow you to see what's going on in your neighborhood. Oh sure, maybe you lack some privacy and backyard decks provide that. But you know what? Front porches are coming back. Dad and I love our front porch that we had screened in 1997 to keep bugs out. This was even better than the original cement slab and posts. We can gossip about neighbors and still enjoy the outside and watch birds at the feeder.

Back to the 1940's in Dorchester a neighbor mom was verbally and physically abusive to her son, the oldest of three kids and was often heard yelling at her husband too. My friends and I who occasionally played with her daughter worried about the mom's sudden explosive ways although sometimes the mom was pleasant as well. Some 14 years later, I met up with this woman sitting on the front porch of her family home, still very obese and now blind and diabetic. She needed help, she said tearfully, to get through each day.

My Friend Ruthie and Our Pre-Teen Years

Okay, I know you can hardly wait for more childhood stories so here they are. At Halloween we did not do the "trick or treat" thing; I don't even remember it as a kid. Maybe that came later or maybe it was just not done in my neighborhood. Halloween night for my friend Ruthie and me meant dressing up in our mother's old coats with fur collars, smearing lipstick on our mouths (that was a big deal) and walking along Blue Hill Avenue eating sour pickles bought from the local deli's big pickle barrel! That was our Halloween celebration! Ruthie remembers us being chased by two boys on one Halloween.

One summer at Revere Beach's amusement park, Ruthie and I went on the Ferris Wheel. We were maybe 12 or 13 and were enjoying our ride when the operator suddenly stopped the wheel, leaving us high in the air. Amused at first, and then frightened, we yelled to him to bring us down. "Was that fun?" he asked, when we reached street level. Without answering and relieved to feel the ground under our feet, we were quick to leave that ride.

When we weren't on Ferris Wheels or eating sour pickles, we were reading love stories in romance magazines or looking at movie magazines. Or else Ruthie and I would gossip about who was the "bleached blonde" and who was the "natural blonde." The dark roots revealed the truth. Today the darkened roots are a must for most fashion-conscious women. I guess we longed to look like the movie stars of the day—Gene Tierney, Donna Reed, Ingrid Bergman—they were some of my favorites. Who could resist Ingrid Bergman in "Casablanca?" So as teens we were concerned with how we looked. I felt I was skinny and flat chested. One of my friends didn't like photos of herself as a child or young teen, so every time we had pictures of ourselves, she crumpled her face in the photo. And she was fast— before I could say "no, no," the photo was crumpled. Silly.

I don't remember doing much homework in elementary school. Maybe we did it all in school. Guess what subject we were graded in? Penmanship—does any teenager today even know what that means? Well, it is hand*writing*—what kids today call "cursive"—that was the first written stuff we learned. Each desk in the classroom had a filled inkwell in the upper right corner that we used to dip our pens. (Occasionally a mischievous boy poked the long pigtails of the girl seated in front of him into the inkwell. That brought strong punitive action from the teacher.) Anyway, no ballpoint pens then—always the pen and ink plus pencil of course. Only later did we learn to print—I remember using stencils a lot to perfect lettering or to make highlights for a geography assignment.

And how did my friends and I make decisions about "firsties," that is, which one of us would go first in a game? Well, of course—we'd "buck up," picking evens or odds and the winner went first. My grandkids—Sam, Max, Jake, Joey and Rachel—you know this one.

At home in Dorchester, my brother and I liked to entertain our parents by presenting our account of "The Shadow Knows," a weekly radio mystery at the time. We'd turn off the lights and then hide behind the parlor curtain to narrate a tale of fear and drama. Our acting talents didn't go much further—although I did have a small part in my senior high school play "Our Town" by Edna Ferber and George S. Kaufman. That was fun. I only had a few lines but my big challenge was to catch an apple tossed from a player across the stage. I was successful. My high school play photo is in the Photo Section.

Drive-In Movies

Drive-in-movies were popular after World War II. We kids would all jump into the back seat of my father's station wagon and hide under blankets and upholstery samples to get in at the lower family rate. For young people dating in those days, a little romance could take place in the darkened car at the drive-in movie. In the late 1950's when the "car culture" had begun, there were over 4,000 drive-in-theatres in America; today there are almost none. Soda fountains were fun; at the corner drug store Ruthie and I would sit and devour our hot fudge sundaes—that was a real treat after school. Here are a few statistics: In 1945 movies for adults cost you 35c, a loaf of bread 8c and a quart of milk 13c. You could buy a new car in 1949 for about $1,800 and a new home with a basement for $10,500.

Junior High School and After

I remember my lunch periods during junior high school. Miss Brennan, one of the teachers was usually the lunchroom supervisor. She was a tall skinny drink of water and she was mean too. I don't think she ever smiled. She'd stand with one hand on her hip and if she thought a behavior was out of place, she would point with her long skinny finger to the offending pupil and say "You...out" which meant to the hallway. (School kids in those days were pupils, not students.) We were all kind of afraid she might see us "misbehave" and we'd whisper about her.

Teachers were a lot stricter when I was growing up. I remember one 6th grade teacher, a Miss Rosonofsky who, despite her severe limp, was tough and demanding. One time my brother Don said a "naughty word." Don doesn't remember what it was but Miss Rosonofsky had him wash his mouth with soapy water. Today that would be considered abusive and a teacher would be reprimanded for it—maybe even dismissed. Teachers back then were permitted to physically punish a student for misbehavior. Today I think that is forbidden in almost every school district.

When we were kids, my parents took out savings accounts for Don and me. I remember the insurance man coming to our home to collect like $1.59 per child per month. Can you imagine this?! How our society has changed! This ended at age 21 when I received the total savings for all those years. I don't remember the amount but it was given to me with great pride by my parents who had saved small amounts each month for the insurance man who came to our home.

How Times Have Changed!

To think that someday we could sit at a keyboard to make a bank deposit or pay our bills was unheard of. Grandpa Eisman certainly would be amazed. There were no credit cards, no ATM money machines, no internet, no fax machines, no cell phones and certainly no video games at that time. I'm reminded of what we'd say if someone suggested, for example, that we'd someday get money from a machine—why that was preposterous! "That is as likely to happen as landing a man on the moon!" Who could know then that a man, Neill Armstrong *would* land on the moon in 1969?!

In my world and my generation, at least as kids in elementary school, we didn't have options of so many sports and other activities away from home. But I did bike a lot. My memory is we came home from school, had something to eat, played outside or in a friend's house until hearing our mom hollering our name signaling it was time to come home for supper. Then we ate supper with our family, did homework, listened to the radio, talked on the phone (we did a lot of that), and went to bed. Of course, no TV then. I do remember my visits to a school chum who lived a mile or so away from our house. Arlene Mindes was a huge fan of Benny Goodman and other big band musicians—it was fun listening to Arlene passionately explain their music to me. Then we'd play records and tap our feet to the rhythm.

Planning Ahead

My brother Don was accepted into Boston Latin School, which was a lot harder than other public schools; it was a big deal to be a student there. He had the brains in the family. I took two years of Latin in junior high and got good grades but that was enough for me—though I did like Mr. Dolan, my Latin teacher. French was more to my liking. Don was accepted and graduated cum laude from Harvard with an English major and got his Master's Degree in Journalism from Columbia University.

Being raised in a traditional home in the 1950's, I had planned on becoming a secretary after high school, encouraged by my parents, especially my father as a good job for a girl whose main goals were to get married, cook a good *gedempte flesh* (pot roast) and have children. After attending Boston University and earning more than a year's credits, I took a job as a legal secretary and then three years later I married Dad. With almost three years of college credits obtained later at the University of Iowa and the University of Minnesota, I finished up at Metropolitan State University and finally got my BA degree in Child Development and Family Relations in 1974 at age 39! It is hard to remember the teenager I was—with a narrow path ahead of me and my role in life scripted by my upbringing—and who I am today. I have learned a lot!

```
  E  /    /
     /   /
     /    /
```

Chapter Fourteen
OUR "ECONOMICAL" FAMILY

Prudent With Money

I want to tell you a bit about my parents' care with their money. My mother was thrifty—"economical" she used to say, and my father encouraged us all to watch what we spent. A lot of people lost money and jobs during the depression; many lost their life's savings—and so that experience had great impact on my parents who tried to save whatever money was left over after essentials. As I mentioned earlier, my mother was a seamstress before she married my father and her skill was in use every place in our home. All my clothes were homemade when I was a child, from coats and dresses, to pajamas and more. Curtains and slipcovers were homemade as well; my mother often purchased remnants to save money. She was proud of her remnant purchase, especially if it was a handsome piece of fabric or a colorful summer print. I remember as a restless kid standing on a chair as my mother measured for the hem on a dress she was making for me. "Stand still," she'd shout many times as she tried with her ruler to chalk or pin the material for a straight hem. Always sewing, Grandma Eisman made draperies for my father's business, off and on over the years.

During the 1930's – 1950's, that was the familiar sight when I came home from school—my mother sewing away on her old Singer with her foot pushing the treadle (years later this Singer was electrified) but still it remained Grandma Eisman's favorite machine. Then when she had finished sewing, everything was put in its place and the machine covered with—what else?—her blue flowery home sewn cover that went down to the floor.

My mother was very particular about her sewing. To assure the best fit, she often basted before the final stitching. For you non-sewers, this does not mean "basting or moistening your roast chicken!" Basting in sewing means to sew loosely with large single thread stitches to temporarily hold fabric together. Then after another fitting you sew the final stitching and then remove the basting thread. So that's a big extra step that insures a perfect fit

How to Be Thrifty in One Easy Lesson

Grandma Eisman was good at patching clothing and recycling things. When towels started to thin, they were sewn into smaller sizes or washcloths. Sheets starting to thin were sewn into pillow cases. Covers or quilts as we called them were woolen blankets covered with cotton print material. They were held in place with safety pins! The homemade cover could be laundered and the same woolen blanket, after hung out on the porch to air, used again. When the covers became worn, my mother made aprons from any sturdy leftover material. If a towel was rendered useless, it was of course transformed into a *shmatteh* (rag); there were no paper towels when I was a kid—always a rag—or if there were paper towels, I never saw them in our home. Holes in socks were always mended on a stocking ball. I too mended socks years ago. When I asked Dad one day when folding laundry why I never see holes in his socks anymore, he told me he tosses them. So Grandma Eisman's stocking ball sits on our dining room buffet—sort of an antique now. People don't mend things these days anymore. We are a "throw away society." Can you imagine one-time use cameras? I admit they are useful if someone forgets a camera and wants to capture a special moment. And now I hear they are working on one-time use camcorders!

When you think that computers need to be replaced every few years or telephones become outdated—why, that's ridiculous. If it works, why replace it? I guess I still have some of the values instilled in me by my parents. I must admit though that sometimes, if I object to a new appliance or gadget and Dad insists on getting it, I do grow to like it! When David was an infant, I worked part-time for a few months and Dad worked at home for the few hours I was gone. One day I came home and there in the laundry room was a brand new clothes dryer. I had been hanging diapers outside on a clothesline to get them fresh and dry. But it took only days for me to fall in love with my new clothes dryer!

Now back to Grandma Eisman's thrifty habits. At breakfast time, to save on paper, my mother would tear the paper napkin in half for each of us (we got a whole napkin for supper!) Chewing gum in my family meant we each had one-half of a stick—a *shtikel* (small piece) for two people—kids and adults alike. If an item purchase were deemed unnecessary, my parents or a relative would say *aroysgevorfen gelt* (useless purchase or literally, money thrown out). (I remember as a kid hearing that my paternal grandmother thought buying a brand new rug and then walking on it was kind of *meshuggeh* (crazy)!)

As I write all of this, I realize there was a lot of emphasis on careful spending and saving money and that actually was the way it was. There was no health insurance or dental insurance and nothing a young family could really fall back on and I guess the hardships of the great depression were a strong memory. Still most of my friends and their parents seemed to be freer about spending money so it was my parents' choice for us to live frugally. Only when you turned 65 could you then count on social security to help in your old age.

It was when my parents turned 65 that they first applied for and purchased health insurance—Blue Cross and Blue Shield—after pressure from me to do this. Prior to that when my father needed hernia surgery in the 1950's, he had to pay the full amount from his savings—I think the hospital and doctors' bills came to almost $10,000.

Keeping House: Woman's Work

Everything got ironed in my mother's world—underwear, pajamas, even towels and washcloths and more—my mother used to say she couldn't put these things into a drawer unless they were ironed plus she found ironing relaxing. (I surely didn't inherit this enjoyment of ironing.) Monday was washday and using her washboard and the kitchen sink, Grandma Eisman got the weekly clothes washed and hung on our porch. My mother wanted clothes hung in fresh air even though in mid winter they froze—which meant spreading them on radiators to thaw and dry. In late afternoon, using a Pepsi Cola bottle with holes in the cap, she sprinkled water on the clothes to be pressed later that night. No steam irons back then. Caps with holes for Pepsi bottles that were used for sprinkling were sold at the Five and Dime Stores (Kresge's and Woolworth's) and indeed did cost a nickel or a dime. These stores were the Targets of our day except there were no checkout lanes. You paid your money to the "sales girls" (I don't remember sales boys), behind the counter who used the cash registers (I remember the clinking) of the day.

Anyway, while listening to the Lux Radio Theatre on Monday nights, my mother ironed the family clothes for the week. Keeping house and raising kids in those days required a lot more physical work than today. My mother was pretty amazed years later when she saw fresh clean diapers delivered to our door—and soon after disposable diapers. "The young people today have it easy," she'd say. "I used to wash and boil in a big pot on the burner two dozen diapers every day— before rinsing and hanging on the back porch line to dry." Now that was a chore!

Grandma Eisman, the *Balebosteh* (Capable Homemaker)

My mother was the true *balebosteh* (housewife, capable homemaker)—it was a compliment. (The male counterpart is the *balebos,* owner of a shop or an orderly person who tended to things). My mother kept an immaculate home, getting up on a kitchen chair or table to wash walls at springtime cleaning. No *shmutz* (dirt) in my parents' home. And I, the daughter, was expected to help with the cleaning. It seems Grandma Eisman never waited for things to look grubby; she had a cleaning schedule and simply followed it.

Every two weeks the inside of the refrigerator needed complete washing, according to my mother. So out would come food, trays and racks to be washed, dried and returned to their proper places. Freezers were not frost-free so the ice built up and had to be thawed, using pans of hot water. I did not like this job; sometimes I faked a stomachache to get out of doing it. Although this was a task, we were far better off than when we had an icebox. Yes, that was the metal box, with double doors that kept your perishables cold. I remember ours was painted yellow and mint green. (Today some people pay loads at antique shops for such an antique.)

Anyway, the iceman would deliver a huge chunk of ice, carried on his back with a huge ice pick stuck into the ice block, up the stairs to our flat. He would deposit it into the ice chest and there it would stay keeping our milk and meat and other foods cold. The large *shissel* (pan) under the ice chest would collect the water that was then dumped, probably a few times a day, much more in summer. It seemed my mother never minded hard physical work—she actually enjoyed it.

After World War II, popular media portrayed homemakers in high heels and fancy hairdos vacuuming their rugs. Not my Ma—she wore her housedress and then an apron for cooking. That was her "uniform" as it was for many other at-home moms of the day. Tossed over my mother's shoulder was the dishtowel—at the ready for wiping hands or removing a hot pot from the oven. Ma didn't have oven mitts—she handily used two ends of the towel to do the job.

Only when going out to bridge or other events or entertaining did Ma change into other clothes. When she needed warmth in winter for her outdoor shopping days, she tucked her housedress into her flannel pants, put on her winter coat and kerchief—always the kerchief—to keep her head warm and off she went. Kerchiefs were very popular in the 1940's—even teens wore them.

Grandma Eisman used to walk a mile or two a few times a week, even in winter, but always with a destination—the grocery store or the post office or to pay a telephone bill. She used to say you needed to swing your arms for maximum benefit and she usually did, that is, until her shopping bags were filled with groceries. She believed physical work helps you stay strong and healthy. My mother wasn't one for long telephone conversations or confrontational issues. She felt "it was her nature" that determined her choices and lifestyle and she often said this about other people as well.

As I write, I realize my tale is filled with "woman's work" in the 1930's and 1940's—but you know, that was the only world I knew. I tried to remember if there were any working moms among my friends. Only an auntie or two who needed to work to supplement the family income come to mind. Otherwise, it was expected that moms raise the kids, do the food shopping, cook the meals, clean their homes and play bridge once a week. As a child, I never questioned the traditional role of women. My father worked hard at his job and built up his upholstery business. Many nights he clearly was exhausted. But he got up again the next morning eager to get to his shop. Lunching with business friends to talk politics and share humor gave him a break and enjoyment. My father was worldlier than my mother—he was generally informed about local politics and foreign affairs and liked discussing the issues of the day.

My mother kept the home clean and neat and fresh looking and saw that my father's suits, shirts and ties were always cleaned, pressed and ready to wear. And my father expected this—after all, that was the woman's role in those days, and my mother took her responsibility seriously.

Store It Away...

My father was a notorious saver—papers, receipts, letters were stored away—as well as old light fixtures, small appliances that didn't work and more. The problem was where to put it. "Store it away," my father would say—he almost never threw anything out. When our Malden home was remodeled in 1949, the old gas light fixtures were stored in the basement. "They'll be worth something someday," my father would say. And he was exactly right because when he died in 1981 and my mother sold the old family house, an antique lady was happy to buy those "wonderful" antique light fixtures. See photo of Malden house in the Photo Section.

My parents were good at repairing things—my mother repaired the frayed and worn cord of her iron knowing which wire went where; and my father had his unique and simple way of making things work again—a piece of wood glued to balance the living room lamp, for example or a cord to hold things together. If it works, why replace it— that was his view? I know my mother often would have preferred a new replacement but my father had the final say. My parents never had air-conditioning in their old 3-story Malden house until Dad and I bought them a window unit for their living room in the 1970's. My father used to say, "It's summer…you have to expect to be hot." They used an electric fan to blow the hot air around in their kitchen. As a kid, I don't remember anyone having air-conditioning in his or her home. The movie theatre or the department store provided the wonderful cool relief from the intense heat of a summer day. Oh, how good that felt!

Fast Forward to 1960's and Beyond: Grandpa Eisman, Communism/Socialism and Russia

I want to say something here about my father's interest in socialism, even communism as a viable alternative to capitalism. This surprised me. Maybe it was the great depression of 1929 and the hardships that followed that triggered Grandpa Eisman's interest in socialism or communism—as a real option to our American capitalism. Several times Grandpa Eisman talked with Dad and me about an economic system like socialism or communism as being a fairer, more equal system for all people; the poorest of citizens should have adequate food and shelter and comfort just like the middle and upper classes. Maybe his views were influenced by sympathy he felt for the Bolsheviks in Russia about the time he and his siblings and mother left the country. Or maybe in a way, he was longing for his old homeland. But he felt a system of government that enables all people to own and share equally in a country's resources and wealth wasn't a bad idea.

Given the fact that Grandpa Eisman was an entrepreneur and proud of it—and he also treasured his privacy, this socialistic view somehow didn't fit. Still, looking back on his remarks, I feel some pride that he cared enough about equality for all people that these economic systems even appealed to him. Of course, his thinking was of an ideal socialist/ communist system. We know Stalin was a dictator. But look at Canada's socialized medicine that works so well. We are the only advanced economy in the world that does not have national health care for all citizens. That's pretty shameful, isn't it? Health care should be a right, just as public school is a right. Hopefully, we will see health care similar to Canada's system or England's health care in our own country when Bush and his cronies are gone. And hopefully, the corporate greed and fraud (Enron, WorldCom, etc.) that has cost ordinary workers and taxpayers their livelihoods and loss of pensions will someday be a thing of the past. Am I dreaming? I hope not. Once or twice Grandpa Eisman asked Dad and me if we would be interested in going to Russia with him and my mother for a visit. But with kids and work plus no dying interest to see Russia, we expressed only mild interest. Obviously, this trip never materialized.

My parents always voted Democratic. I think my father considered voting for Republican Dwight Eisenhower in 1952 because of Eisenhower's (Ike) role in World War II. Ike was everyone's hero then—Dad tells me he was the first and only Five-Star General—and he led the allies to victory in Europe. The Democrats tried to get Ike to run on the Democratic ticket—he was clearly popular. Adlai Stevenson, the Democratic nominee who ran against Eisenhower in both 1952 and 1956, was brilliant and thoughtful and a person of integrity. It was a shame that he was never elected—I think he would have done great things for our country. I cast my first presidential vote for Stevenson in 1956 when I was 22. Voting age was 21 in those days. It was the early 1970's when the voting age was dropped to 18.

Chapter Fifteen
MORE on FOOD: WHAT ELSE?

Going Shopping (Not at the Mall)

In every "good" Jewish home, food was king. What one ate, is eating or will eat was the highlight of the day. As in many homes, food was what bonded our family together. My mother was a great cook; her food shopping and cooking were the two things she loved doing. She hated shopping for clothes—but food shopping—that was her pleasure. Today when I hear women say they are "going shopping," I know they mean the mall for clothes and accessories. For Ma, that meant grabbing her shopping bag and heading down the hill on Greenock Street to the fruit store or the meat market.

Blue Hill Avenue in Dorchester was a bustling Jewish neighborhood in the 1940's. There were no supermarkets then, so shopping for your family meant many stops. The fruit store might be first, then the grocery store, onto the meat market, maybe the fish market and lastly the bakery for fresh breads. Milk in glass bottles was delivered to your door—that was convenient. In early years a horse and carriage carried bottled milk to your home. The famous G & G Delicatessen on Blue Hill Avenue, a symbol of Jewish Dorchester closed in the 1970's

Fresh produce was eaten or cooked shortly after purchasing it to "get the most nutrition." We didn't think about harmful pesticides or chemicals in our fruits and vegetables. I think our produce back then was fresher than today with far less chemicals. In the past 30 years according to David Pimentel et al in the 1989 journal *Bioscience*, there has been an increase of 20% more insecticides used in our produce. Of course, we grow more crops to feed more people but the insecticides are used, in addition to keeping crops from becoming pest infested, to make produce more cosmetically appealing. Today more and more consumers are demanding organic foods, if they can afford it. I hope the higher prices come down—this would certainly be environmental equality—organic foods for everyone, not only those who can afford to buy it.

There was nothing rotted or old in my mother's refrigerator when I was a kid. If a fruit was overly ripe, my mother would insist that we all have a taste "before it gets spoiled." Hard bread was crushed into breadcrumbs. If a bit of food from dinner was left in the pot or plate, my mother would say, "it's a shame to throw it out…people are starving around the world…finish it." And we did. Serving portions were modest; I don't remember huge, heavy meals or people over-eating. So despite the emphasis on food in our families, diets were healthy and sensible—that is, if you discounted the chicken fat that was cooked in some meals!

Grandma Eisman encouraged eating fresh fruit and in-season summer fruit especially. She'd pass fresh cold and washed fruit whenever anyone sat around the kitchen table or in the living room. Often with the fruit sat a bowl of *semishkes* (Russian for sunflower seeds in shells)—this was a family *nosh* (snack).

Table Conversation: Israel and Palestine— Hope for the Future

Conversation at the table revolved around family and events. Among the men in our extended family the talk was about business, politics and the like. Our families were concerned with and supported the development of the state of Israel though they were not activists in this regard. Our mothers were members of Hadassah, a women's volunteer organization dedicated to the support and delivery of education and social services to all people in Israel. Today Hadassah Hospitals and Medical Center is one of the prime medical research centers in the world.

And now, after so long, we yearn for peace for Israelis and Palestinians. With the absence of Prime Minister Ariel Sharon and the newly elected Hamas majority, the future is less clear. Sharon initiated the dismantling of the settlements in Gaza, a difficult and emotional process. Seeing the faces of Israelis being moved from their homes and their synagogues by unarmed Israeli military whose job it was to complete this process showed that this exit from Gaza was a big sacrifice. Still, I feel the dismantling of the settlements is the best chance for peace for both the Israelis and the Palestinians. Establishing an independent Palestine will make for a safer and more secure Israel. And a safe and secure and permanent Israel is in the best interests of the Palestinians—if only Hamas would realize this. As I write today, the United States and the European Union have demanded that Hamas renounce violence and recognize Israel's right to exist. Such sorrow and sadness for so many people on both sides. Americans for Peace Now (APN) and its Israeli counterpart Shalom Achshav (PEACE NOW) are recognized in our country and in Israel as the premier peace movement and one that I strongly support. I hope and pray that soon a fair and just agreement can be reached for both the Israelis and the Palestinian people.

Heymishe (Informal, Warm and Cozy) Family Gatherings

So I guess when I look back on my childhood, my most Jewish experience was in the food my mother and my Auntie Rose cooked up and the *heymishe* (warm and cozy and home-like) setting in which we enjoyed it. But our family cooks weren't the "gourmet" types in the sense that having new pots and pans mattered. We couldn't afford them anyway, and if a lid fit, use it—doesn't matter what it goes to. In my mother's kitchen, food was cooked in old enamel pots but never with inside bruises. She did have a big roaster to roast up a couple chickens or a brisket for company dinner. And then there was the heavy aluminum cooker for simmering *gedempte flaish* (pot roast), a cooker that I use today. Cooked with the *gedempte flaish* was the marrow, carefully removed from the bone and offered to children to give them brains. I actually liked it—that's probably why I am so smart!

Our mothers handled food lovingly—a bowl of fruit or a whole chicken—was handled with care and respect. And hard work went into preparing a meal. An old hand grinder was used to grind raw beef for *Chaluptses (*Stuffed Cabbage), meat loaf or hamburger. Only later did our mothers purchase ground meat from the butcher. Today we lucky cooks can buy ground fish for Passover and ground meats of all kinds.

Grandma Eisman's Meal Planning "System"

Ma, as we called my mother, had a routine or as she called it a "system" for buying and serving meals to our family. She felt this was the way to insure "variety" and a healthy diet. You could expect certain meals with some variation on certain days of the week. Of course, Friday night was always chicken, followed by soup. Saturday's dinner was the bigger meal of the day (usually Friday night's leftover dinner heated). In Orthodox Jewry, "lighting" the stove during the Sabbath was forbidden so Friday's leftovers, unheated, were eaten. This practice was carried over in the not-so Orthodox homes like ours. However, my mother did "light" the stove to heat the meal. "Make the stove" was my mother's expression rather than "turn on the oven" probably from olden days when you literally had to make the fire. Supper at night might be smoked fish with potatoes or in summer *shav* (sorrel or cold grass) with sliced cucumber. *Shav* is actually Russian, not Yiddish. Cold beet borscht with a dollop of sour cream was another favorite. (See Recipes in the Recipe Index.)

Sunday dinner (actually it was the lunchtime meal) was later than usual because breakfast was more filling and was eaten later in the morning. If I had plans for Sunday (movies, etc.) it was to be either before or after the Sunday dinner. Neither Don nor I ever asked that my mother refrigerate our dinner so we could eat when we got home—the Sunday family dinner together was important in our family and we were expected to be there for it. Sometimes I envied the freedom of my friend Ruthie for whom these rules didn't apply, but I never questioned our family's Sunday dinner tradition.

The *forshpeiz* (appetizer) might be freshly grated horseradish with a bit of red onion tossed with *schmaltz* (chicken fat) and topped with cut up cucumber—or chopped egg with onion—or my favorite: pickled herring. My mother pickled her own herring for years. I used to sneak downstairs at night to eat a piece or two; it was the best—I wish I could come up with a recipe for it.

There was always bread—good crusty bread with fresh garlic rubbed into the crusts, a bit of salt—that was great. Standard was the Challah on Friday nights and rye breads and *bulkes* (rolls) and *pletsels* (a sort of thin flat crisp roll, often topped with onion and poppyseed) on other nights.

Thanksgiving in my parents' home did not mean turkey. It might mean *gensel* (soft "g" and meaning goose; I don't know if *gensel* is Yiddish or Russian). That pleased my father greatly—I think he liked the sound as well as the taste of *gensel* because he'd repeat it a few times before and during the meal.

Conversation around the table was light, although in later years in Malden, when my parents weren't getting along, the mood was tense; I didn't like it. I always felt the burden to cheer things up. But my early years in Dorchester were happier around the table. Someone was always telling what my father called a *"leingeh meyseh"* pronounced with soft "g" and *meyseh* rhyming with icy (meaning long story). If my father was pressed to do or tell something unpleasant, he'd answer in half Yiddish/half English *Vos is on anderer* station/channel? (What is on the other station/channel?), meaning he wanted to change the subject. Or if someone would kid my mother and she knew it, she'd say, *"Hak mir nisht kain tsheinik"* (Don't bother me; literally don't bang on the tea kettle)—this expression is one of my favorites, and I think kind of reflects the color and character of the Yiddish language.

Of course, Grandpa Eisman began the meal as many Europeans did with the *schnapps* downed with one gulp; my mother and grandmother and other adult relatives present joined in. First the *l'chaim* (to life) followed by the chaser of cold seltzer water from a siphon. The siphon was a huge and heavy glass bottle with a metal siphon attached. The water was very bubbly—never went dead—I guess because of the way it was sealed and the siphon thing. My father loved this ritual and he so enjoyed my mother's cooking. These siphons of seltzer water were actually delivered every week or two in Malden and the empties picked up. Although I didn't drink the seltzer as a kid, I liked depressing the lever and watching the bubbly water pour out. I've been told that some Jewish New York City restaurants still serve siphons of cold bubbly water.

Accompanying dessert was always the cup of hot tea—real hot—that is how the adults liked their tea and soup. I remember my *Bubbe* Kamsky drinking her *glezel tai* (glass of tea). She'd pour small amounts into a saucer and suck tea through a sugar cube held between her incisors. My mother and other relatives, mostly women, also drank their hot tea this way. I guess the sugar cube gave the sweet kick they enjoyed after a meal. In later years, first thing in the morning, my mother drank her cup of hot water and often she too poured the hot boiling water from the cup into a saucer and sipped it that way. No sugar cube though!

All of the cooking and baking in Dorchester was done in the oven of the big black stove with its huge flue vented into the ceiling and then to the outside. My mother hated that stove because it was hard to keep clean, she'd say; today it is sought after for those who want to re-create a kitchen of the past.

Eating Out: A Rare Treat

We rarely ate out in the 1940's but on special occasions, say Mother's Day or my parents' anniversary, we'd drive to 5 Tyler Street in Boston for Chinese food. We'd climb the long flight upstairs to the restaurant, and the wonderful aroma of food made us a lot hungrier. Why Chinese food was and still is popular with Jewish families when eating out beats me. But the food was great. And these events happened on a Sunday so parking was free and easy near downtown Boston. My mother always brought along their small jar filled with whiskey (I think it was Canadian Club rye whiskey) for my father and herself. It was their *schnapps* before dinner and if the waiter happened to see it, my father told him it was their medicine. (I guess it was in a way.) Poured into their teacups and smiling, they would toast their *l 'Chaim* and drink their *schnapps*. Five Tyler Street was our family's favorite place to go; they usually had live music and dancing too. After the meal, it was off to the RKO theatre for live music (I remember Gene Krupa on the drums) plus a comedian and then a movie. This was quite a treat for not more than the price of a movie admission. You got a lot for your money at these RKO movie theatre specials in those days. This Sunday dinner and a show was rare—only on special occasions did our family indulge this way.

I really don't remember doing special dinners out for birthdays. My parents weren't even certain of their own birthdates; I don't think they ever celebrated birthdays in Russia while growing up, or in America. Would you believe they actually had to choose birthdays for themselves when coming to the U.S.? Grandma Eisman said her mother had told her she was born in the heat of summer so she picked August 13th as her birthday. My father's birthday on legal papers was March 4th.

Nourishment and Variety—and Cod Liver Oil!

As I mentioned, my mother believed that variety in food was important. And that meant we all needed prunes one morning a week and that was on Saturday! I dreaded having to eat that as well as hot cooked cereal—again, I think once a week.

Milk was an important food for us. My mother would add Bosco (like chocolate syrup but more nutritious) and occasionally a raw egg (ugh) for "nourishment." No one ever thought about unpasteurized raw eggs making a child sick. Well—that glass of milk sat in front of me for what seemed like hours. You guys are in a modern era but bottled milk in those days was not homogenized which meant the cream would float on the top of the milk and no matter how hard you'd shake to dissolve it, there was always a little cream floating on top. Ugh! When the raw egg was added, it would actually make me sick, so if my mother looked the other way, I'd quick pour most of the milk down the drain! Also, you kids and grandkids are lucky to have a candy coated vitamin pill or sweet tasting syrup, but we had to swallow "cod liver oil!" This was oil from the liver of codfish and other fish and had a lot of Vitamins A and D. Suppose to be good for you. God, that was awful!

Not food related—but tending to injuries in the 1930's and 1940's meant one of two antiseptics would be applied after the soap and water cleansing. If a cut or scrape was minor, you were lucky to get the mild red mercurochrome (nothing to do with mercury). But if the cut was deeper or more serious, oh, oh—then you got the iodine, a deep orange colored antiseptic that was stronger and harsher. Boy, did that sting!

Chapter Sixteen
A TWO-PARTY TELEPHONE LINE:
for a FRUGAL HOUSEHOLD
and MORE STORIES

Get Off the Phone! Now!

A two-party telephone line, which was the least expensive type and offered limited service, was the one we had growing up in Dorchester in the 1930's and 1940's. This meant that two families who usually did not know each other shared the telephone line so that if one family talked on the phone when one of us wanted to make a call, we'd pick up the receiver (it was called that) and hear people talking. The other party line might yell, "Get off the phone!" Sometimes these conversations were interesting and you could sneak a listen but usually the party line heard the click and knew you were listening. Anyway, this limited service meant that calling even into downtown Boston was "an extra call" and so we almost never called into Boston unless really necessary. Phone calls to relatives to wish them—*Gott Yontiff* (Good Holiday), for example, or wish them well on a trip were very brief ending with *gai gezunterheit* (bon voyage or good-bye—literally go in good health). Telephoning was more costly back then. Today you get a lot of minutes for your money.

At my father's upholstery shop, the phone service was also limited—only a minimum number of calls were allowed—again a money saver, this time for the business. So what did Grandpa Eisman do when he needed to call home? He'd call, let the phone ring twice and hang up.

This was the signal to my mother to return his call that was allowed in our low-cost system, so she did just that and the conversation was completed.

Mr. Greenstein, Our Boarder at 41 Greenock Street

When we were kids in Dorchester, my parents took in a boarder, a Mr. Greenstein for extra income. He was an older bachelor (I think he worked in insurance), a pleasant person who occasionally ate with us but mostly he heated his Campbell's Chicken noodle soup and ate it with VB sardines and Uneeda biscuits or his *bulke* (roll). When my mother discovered "girlie" magazines in his closet while cleaning his room, she and my father immediately asked him to leave. I don't know what they said to him but his departure was swift but friendly. My mother later told me she and my father decided to ask him to leave because I was "a growing girl" and I guess somehow she connected his "leisure reading" with me!

Tending the Furnace in Dorchester

Tending the furnace for our flat in Dorchester ("flat" from the British influence) was gender neutral in our family. All of us were responsible for adding coal to the furnace and stoking it, removing the ashes and storing them in a barrel. We'd have to cautiously open the furnace door (it was very hot) and there into the blazing fire, we tossed two, three, sometimes more shovelfuls of coal to keep the furnace going in the dead of winter.

Don and I were just kids in our pre or early teens but taught to be careful and responsible in helping to keep the furnace going. (Each of the 3 flats in the house had its own furnace and small storage area.) Then the very heavy barrel loaded with ashes from the furnace was taken up a few steps and kind of turned out on its base and moved to the front of the house where it was picked up by the city once a week. It was work in those days to heat your home in winter. There were no thermostats, at least not in our home at the time, that, with the flick of your finger, warmed your home. If you wanted heat, you did the work and when the radiators warmed to the touch—ah, that felt nice. You knew the heat was working.

The rent for our flat was $33 a month. I was responsible for bringing the cash upstairs to Mrs. Kopel, our landlady. Mrs. Kopel did not like our friends climbing the nice big tree in our back yard. *"Gai avek!"* (Go away!), she would holler and if we did not, she would throw buckets of water on us to get us off the tree! Years later in 1963 when Dad, David, Pam and I (Joel, you were not yet born) revisited my old Dorchester neighborhood, the tree had been cut down. The tree may have been shattered by a storm, neighbors told us. What a shame!

The "triple decker" or three-story, three-family, flat-topped structure in which we lived was typical of Dorchester, Massachusetts. I recently read that more than 5,000 of these were built in Dorchester between 1900-1925. The flats were of good size and included, as I mentioned earlier, front and back porches. They were built to give low and moderate-income families the benefits of suburban-type living and the convenience of living near their jobs.

A Bit of "Bawstin" Accent

I want to say something about my *Bawstin* accent that I guess I've still got, though it's now mixed with a midwestern flavor. You kids had some of my Boston accent when you were preschoolers but quickly lost it when you started school. So for those of you who want it, here's the short version: Dropping the "r" is major and substituting an "h" for the "r." That's how *"park the car in Harvard Yard"* becomes *"pahk the cah in Havid Yahd."* My cousin Dorothy recently e-mailed me saying, "Aren't you *'mahvelous'* to be so close to finishing your book!" So even Bostonians make fun of their own accent.

Okay, then you have the "ah's" to contend with as in *bahth or hahf.* And lastly, eating the *"lobster roll"* becomes eating the "lobsta roll" *stahting* first with the clam *chowdah.* Conversely, if one's name ends in "a" as in *Roberta,* well, she becomes *Roberter*! Go figure! By the way, you know—Boston has long been famous for their baked beans—that's why Boston is called "Beantown."

_A_/__/__
__/__/__
__/__/__

Chapter Seventeen
RESPECT for PARENTS and ELDERS: THE RIGHT THING to DO

Obedience and Politeness Matter

My brother Don and I were raised to be polite, obedient kids, taught to defer to our parents and other adults—for example, teachers and "policemen" and the like and that is what we did. We knew when we disobeyed because one look from my father told us we'd better shape up. Actually, I vaguely remember as a kid that a strap hung somewhere in the house that my father once or twice referred to—but he never used it.

My mother scolded us by having us stand in the corner, face to the wall until she felt we had "learned our lesson and would not do that misbehavior again." Sometimes when topics like money, family problems or death were discussed, Don and I were sent out of the room by our father. Our family setting was "adult oriented" and we kids needed to "know our place." I later resented this but I respected my parents' traditions and behaved accordingly. (It has just occurred to me that I remember my father saying once or twice when someone had acted out of line that he would "give that person a call-down." I never liked that expression that implied a big scolding or a "put-down." Fortunately, I heard it only rarely.) Do well in school, work hard, save your money, listen to parents, help and care for family, respect elders and obey traditions and customs—these were the values passed down to Don and me. My parents respected hard work. Those who took pride in their craft and worked at it diligently were admired.

One family expectation was that I marry a Jewish boy. And so I mostly dated Jewish boys. Dating and marrying in the Jewish religion was an expectation for many young Jewish girls in the 1950's. Many Jewish teens were expected to conform and I was no exception. I did date a nice non-Jewish young man, a lawyer whom I had met at work but I kept this from my parents. In high school, however, I was close friends with Arthur Mouradjian, a warm and friendly guy who gave me rides to school many mornings. We went to the senior prom together in 1951 and then to the Latin Quarter with other classmates to hear Patti Paige (she's still singing). Though Arthur was not Jewish, my parents fully accepted this relationship—I guess they realized it was not a romantic one and they were correct.

Looking Back

I talked earlier about following customs and traditions as a child and as a teen and so I did. I don't remember being present at a *Brit* or *Bris* (the Jewish ceremony of circumcision) when I was growing up although I must have been because I have younger cousins who are boys. This is an important tradition for most Jews and I was proud and happy to be present at the *Brises* of my four wonderful grandsons. But—and I know this may shock some of my more Conservative or Orthodox relatives, I knew when my own sons were born that I did not want such a ceremony. Dad and I both wanted the circumcision for our sons, but neither of us wanted the ceremony. Because both sets of grandparents lived a long distance, there was no one close by to object to our decision—and so a medical doctor circumcised both our sons in the hospital. Our infants were then immediately brought to us where they were nursed and nurtured and adored. It is the idea of people gathered in the room while the procedure is done that bothers me—I have great difficulty in celebrating this way. Yes, the tradition is rich and significant and is a covenant with God and I honor those who wish to have the traditional *Bris.* Fortunately, in this area Dad and I agree.

Medical research has shown that there are important public health benefits in circumcision. Besides the hygienic advantages gained by having this procedure, circumcision has been shown to lessen heterosexual transmission of the HIV virus and there may be evidence that it can lessen the chance of cervical cancer for women. Today circumcision is widespread in the United States although, to be sure, there are some who oppose it.

Adolescence—So Long Ago

It was in the late 1940's at Revere Beach when I was about 12 or 13 that I became interested in boys. It was fun flirting and splashing in the ocean with Jerry Napoleon and Sheldon Lilly. Sheldon tragically was killed in a car crash while on furlough during the Korean War.

My friend Ruthie and I liked boys and concocted ways to meet them. Once I called a boy whose picture I saw and liked in my brother's high school yearbook and made up some kind of story about how I knew him. I invited him to a "house party" and asked him to bring friends. His name was Jerry Saunders. We liked each other and dated for many months. Later, I introduced one of his close friends to my friend Wilma who later became her husband. George is a medical doctor and he and Wilma have four kids and grandkids and have been happily married for over 50 years! Today these shenanigans (calling strange boys on the phone) would surely be foolish and maybe even dangerous. Somehow things seemed a lot safer in those days.

I had several boyfriends through my junior high and high school years. One guy I dated awhile was Jack Pinkovitz whose name I remember well because, fast-forwarding to the 1980's when my mother and Auntie Rose lived in Sharon, it so happened my Auntie Rose was an overnight babysitter for Jack and his family. So some 40 years after we dated, Jack and his two kids visited me at my mother's home in Sharon. Jack was tall and smiled easily; as planned he had become an engineer after graduating from MIT. And there he was, sweaty from sailing with his kids that afternoon, in my mother's living room as we reminisced and updated each other on our lives. One thing sticks out in my mind—I remember in the early 1950's when we dated that his friend's wife or girlfriend couldn't double date with us because it was the girl's "hair-washing" night! Unbelievable, isn't it?

But you know shampooing one's hair or even bathing or showering was not a daily thing back then. Growing up, many of us—Dad tells me this was so in his home—had **weekly** baths unless something special was going on. Yes—that's true. I guess in "olden times," as my mother used to say, filling a bathtub with hot water was an event—I don't ever remember my mother filling the tub so one could soak in it—there was just enough water to wash one's body. Aren't we lucky to have fresh and abundant water so accessible? We must conserve and appreciate what we take for granted every day. And we must work to see that all families have a fresh and safe water supply.

Anyway, another high school relationship was with Aaron Levine who lived over 30 minutes away. Aaron had no car and so took the streetcar to pick me up for our dates. He's pictured with me at my high school graduation in the Photo Section. I still have the rhinestone jewelry set he gave me—all four pieces probably in good condition. Vintage jewelry now—I think I'll check it out with an outfit soon.

In those years "going steady" meant you had one boyfriend—and only one—whom you were dating. Lou Barker, for example, a friendly and really nice guy gave me an option when I was about 16: either he or I were to become more serious, that is, go steady—or stop seeing each other. I chose the latter and sadly said good-bye. I remember that time well as we sat in his car; I had just had a penicillin shot for strep throat and felt awful plus I worried I'd get him sick too. I never saw him after that. There were other boyfriends in my late teens and some nice relationships. In the 1950's women were marrying at much younger ages—so I was "looking!" Also there was increasing tension between my parents and it was unpleasant. So I was anxious to get a loving partner and be on my own. Dad answered the call!

My First Look at this Thing Called Television

It was in Malden in 1950 that a school friend Margie Block and her family invited a few of Margie's friends over to watch the Ed Sullivan

Show on television. We all gathered around their tiny 12" black and white TV set. My, what technology then! Despite the frequent poor reception, these new TV sets were fascinating. Do you know that in 1945, most people surveyed didn't know what television was? People in the 1940's hung out in their living rooms in the evenings and listened to their radios.

The next year in 1951 my parents bought their first black and white TV set and they just loved it. "Television sets" in the early days were sold in big mahogany or blond furniture cabinets—not like the single TV one can buy today—thus the term "TV sets." So they were actually a piece of furniture and thought was needed as to where to place it. Television became my parents' nightly recreation as it was for many families in the 1950's—and so it continues.

Would you believe in high school I babysat for 25c an hour? Babysitting was usually at the Pasteurs who had 3 kids. Once in a while with Mrs. Pasteur's permission, I had a boyfriend over to keep me company and together, we watched the Milton Berle show on TV. Today I disapprove of babysitters having boyfriends or girlfriends over while they baby-sit. I guess like in other areas, there are two standards: one—if you are a teenager; and two—if you're in the protective role of a parent or a grandparent.

The Double Standard is Everywhere

The double standard—a different standard of right and wrong for men and women—was present everywhere in the 1930's-1950's. In the newspapers, until even more recently, it was legal to have segregated employment ads—columns for women and columns for men. It seemed "so natural" to treat men and women separately this way. Women in general today earn 75% of what men do. Some of this is different work; some is discrimination. And in many homes the woman is the sole support of her family, particularly in low income families—and so women need greater equality here.

Did you know that when I was growing up it was legal to dismiss pregnant teachers from public school teaching jobs as well as married flight attendants from their jobs? And many in society endorsed these laws and policies. Again, never mind that many of these women needed the income to support their families.

Old traditions continued in my parents' home. As far back as I can remember, my father gave my mother cash for the weekly groceries and other needs. But later in Malden, when she was in charge of collecting the rent from the downstairs neighbor, she opened a savings account to deposit these monthly rent checks. Then she told me "I got smart—if Daddy didn't give me enough money, I took money from the rent account."

Today there is far greater equality between the sexes than when I was growing up in the 1940's and 1950's. Still, despite the great strides made in our country, many challenges remain. Even in 2005 as I write we continue to see evidence of male power in families, in politics, in religion and in employment.

Of course in the area of premarital sexuality, the double standard was a given. Men were permitted, even encouraged, to have sex before marriage. But for women this was a huge no-no. Dad has spent his professional career researching and writing on human sexuality and so you know the issues in this area.

Desegregation in Public Schools

Desegregation in public schools was a huge fight in our country but finally in 1954 the Supreme Court of the United States found that "separate but equal" has no place in American education. Some state legislatures tried but failed to propose laws to abolish this decision.

Still today, despite the law, there are segregated schools, in part due to segregated neighborhoods. In addition, poor neighborhoods often have shamefully shabby broken down school buildings. This is the setting facing millions of children. As my hero, the late U. S. Senator of Minnesota Paul Wellstone described in his 2001 book *The Conscience of a Liberal*: "I have asked senators…how well they would do if we had no air-conditioning during the hot Washington summers, if the heating was inadequate during the winters, if the toilets didn't work…if the roof leaked during rainstorms, if the building was decrepit…these are the conditions facing millions of schoolchildren," he shouted out on the floor of the Senate. "What kind of message do we send these children? We are telling them that we don't value or care about them." Here was a Senator who spoke the truth and worked to actually make a difference in people's lives.

In 1955 the courageous Rosa Parks refused to sit in the back of the city bus in Montgomery, Alabama and then was arrested. Hard to believe, isn't it? Her arrest and aftermath bolstered the Civil Rights Movement. In 1964 the Civil Rights Act made discrimination in employment on the basis of sex, race, color or religion illegal, and President Lyndon Johnson signed it into law. I was never a fan of Lyndon Johnson, but it was under his watch that these major changes began.

Chapter Eighteen
BUBBE FRIEDA EISMAN PASSES AWAY

My Paternal Grandmother, *Bubbe* Frieda Eisman Dies

I knew my paternal grandmother, *Bubbe* Frieda Eisman and visited with her over the years. She was kindly but often seemed sad—perhaps due to her husband's long time out-of-marriage love affair. In the years after coming to America, my father and his siblings lived at home with their mother and contributed a portion of their salaries for family expenses.

That was the custom at the time; adult unmarried children were expected to live in their parents' home until they married—and contribute to the family's upkeep—unless they had moved to another city for school or work. And so I too continued this custom. Young single people of all religions living on their own didn't appear until the late 1960's. Actually, Dad had a graduate student around that time at the University of Iowa who did his Master's Degree thesis on this new phenomenon of young unmarried people living independently.

In my *Bubbe* Frieda Eisman's home, her children (my father and his siblings) were free to come and go as they chose. They were respectful of their mother and knew the established traditions.

Bubbe Frieda Eisman baked wonderful breads and rolls almost daily. Her specialty was the *knishes* recipe (baked rolls filled with meat or potato)—which she often baked when my brother and I were very young. (Though they are both *Bubbe* Eisman, I must remind my kids—

David, Pam and Joel—this is my paternal grandmother—not your maternal grandmother whose story I am telling here.) My mother told me she loved the baked bread aroma from my grandmother's kitchen during the years she and my father courted.

For a number of years later, *Bubbe* Frieda Eisman lived with her daughter, my Auntie Molly and her family. My grandmother, like other immigrant women of her generation from Russia in those years, though fluent in Russian, never really learned to read or write English. I remember that she signed her name with only an "X!" That was legal then. Her "X" probably needed notarization from a Notary Public—I don't remember. I guess the "X" indicated acknowledgement and approval of a document.

In her later years, unhappily, she went to live in "an old-age home." It was sad when my parents and I visited her. The setting was one big room with a bed, a small dresser and a chair or two for each resident lined up against a long wall. And this was the community "bedroom" for maybe twelve or more residents. The surroundings were not warm nor were they cheerful. My *Bubbe* Frieda Eisman talked some, always in Yiddish, to my parents and me and often insisted I have some of her jewelry; she'd say *nem, nem* (take, take)—and I'd look to my father for approval, which was often in agreement with his aged mother.

The Traditional *Shivah*: Eight Days of Mourning

I remember my *Bubbe* Frieda Eisman's death. It was in 1947 and I was in junior high school. Her death was the first in our extended family that I can recall. Many relatives came to sit *shivah* (mourning for the dead beginning immediately after the funeral) at my Auntie Molly's home. The word *shivah* is from the Hebrew meaning "seven" which is the number of days one should mourn in Orthodox Judaism. This practice also requires the covering of mirrors (no vanity at this time) and the burning of the Shivah candle for seven days. To indicate grief in traditional Judaism, the mourner wears an outer garment that has been torn or cut, or the mourner may attach a cut black ribbon to a garment. These tears reflect the broken heart of the mourner at the loss of his or her loved one. The cuts on a garment or a ribbon are rendered differently depending on who is mourning; but for all persons in traditional Judaism, this ceremony is performed standing up to teach us to meet all sorrow standing upright.

In memory of my grandmother and in keeping with the traditional *shivah*, family and friends came to sit *shivah* on hard wooden benches or chairs and recite with our family the *kaddish* (mourners' prayer). In Orthodoxy, this family worship required a *minyan* (quorum of ten men—boys 13 or over could be counted; they generally were bar mitzvahed and were considered young adults). Today female inclusion in the *minyan* is fully accepted in Reform and Conservative Judaism, but still not accepted in Orthodox Judaism.

David and Sue: I read recently what your Rabbi Norman Cohen of Bet Shalom in Minneapolis said in a Temple piece: "The *minyan* is the original support group in history. This is the time that family and friends gather together to recite the *kaddish* and support the bereaved family so this certainly qualifies as a support group," wrote Rabbi Cohen.

Chapter Nineteen
MOVING to MALDEN

Leaving Dorchester for Malden

My father wanted to be nearer to his Melrose business, so in 1949 we moved from Dorchester to Malden into a two-story, two-family home built around the 1900's. I remember my father coming home to tell us that he had just bought the house—my mother had not even seen it yet! That's pretty amazing, isn't it? We knew my parents had been looking for a home in a particular Malden neighborhood but to actually buy it before my mother had seen it, why today I find that incredible. My father was definitely the authority figure in our home and my mother accepted it. But she was happy to make the move. The move meant a new school for me; I had just finished my sophomore year at the all-girls Jeremiah Burke High School and would be a junior at the co-educational Malden High School. Yes! Don was at Boston Latin School (K-12) which meant he did not need to change schools. We were all excited about the move.

My parents went about remodeling the much larger upstairs apartment (with its own two levels) that would be our residence. Grandpa Eisman instructed the electrician to save all old lamps and other old stuff. "They will be worth money someday," he said. And he was right. As I mentioned earlier, some 30 years later when my mother was ready to sell the family home, an antique dealer was happy to purchase all that "old stuff."

Major Remodeling to Our Family Home

The remodeling of the Malden house involved removing some of the beautiful dark woodwork and painting all wooden surfaces white. Glass doors on bookcases were removed and left open—and the shelves painted pale green with white trim to conform to the modern style of smooth open space. It seemed like the thing to do at the time. A nice pantry in the kitchen was also eliminated to make the kitchen larger. Decisions were made with an architect cousin who was knowledgeable and his father who was a top-notch carpenter. Uncle Yissa, the carpenter, though a small man, had big chunky fingers and large hands from his many years of woodworking. Moving quickly, he'd stop to explain what was being done. It was a huge job.

Heavy mahogany wooden room openings were removed and replaced with scalloped arches, which were then wallpapered. And the rest of the dark woodwork upstairs was sanded and painted white. I guess many new homeowners today opt for white woodwork so here we are back again to the 1950's. As for me, I like the look of natural wood. However, I must admit that at the time, the white paint did brighten up the residence of our new Malden home.

My mother liked ceramic tile so the big kitchen got peach tile with black trim. White window shades were the first thing ordered—you needed your privacy as soon as possible. These shades were hung in windows everywhere when I was little. Venetian blinds were more expensive so my parents opted for the shades. Grandma Eisman sewed peach chiffon curtains for the four kitchen windows—they were cute

Pink and blue ceramic tile went into our family bathroom. Small diamond shaped tiles covered the floor—two or three of them were always loose; no glue seemed to hold them in place. And who even knew of more than one bathroom in a four-bedroom house. I don't think we even questioned a big house with only one bathroom. My, things have changed. Also in the late 1940's, wall-to-wall carpeting in your living room and dining room meant you were pretty modern, and so these rooms were carpeted. Today many people remove carpeting and lay down wooden floors. Topping off all this remodeling was an 8-chime doorbell that sounded like church bells. For some reason, Grandpa Eisman loved these chimes.

This move in 1949 meant big changes for my family. Twenty-seven years after coming to the United States, my parents had purchased their own home in a very desirable part of Malden and my father was the owner of a successful upholstery business. Not bad for two Russian immigrants!

Chapter Twenty
OUR WEDDING: SEPTEMBER 4, 1955

Seven Weeks: A Short Engagement—
but a Happy Wedding

"*Ze Gait zein a Chasenah* (There's going to be a wedding)," my mother said to my grandmother, *Bubbe* Kamsky, on a hot July morning in 1955. "Harriet and Ira are getting married in September."

"*Mazeltov!* (Congratulations!; literally lucky day)," exclaimed my grandmother. I took the phone. "*Vos makst du, Bubbe?* (How are you Grandma?)," I asked. I pictured my *Bubbe* sitting at the table having her *glezel tai* (glass of tea). Bubbe and I talked a bit, me in my broken Yiddish and laughed together. "*Ira is zayre klug* (very smart)," my *Bubbe* said. "*Gariez* (Greetings) to him."

"*Zeit gezunt* (Be well)", I said and hung up.

There was a lot to do to get ready for a September wedding. First was my parents' invitation to the new *machutonim* (in-laws). The dinner probably included chopped liver, chicken soup, roast chicken and kasha and varnishkes (Recipes in Recipe Index). My parents wanted to make the evening festive for my expectant in-laws, starting with the *schnapps* and the *l'chaim* (to life) toast—My *Bubbe* Kamsky joined us for this happy occasion.

Dad and I met in late January 1955 and were engaged in July and married on September 4th of the same year. I needed to quit my job as legal assistant to Reuben Landau and that was difficult because I had promised him I'd be working through the summer when his secretary took her vacation. But we were able to make last minute arrangements to keep his office covered. (This highly regarded Boston lawyer was still living and practicing law in Boston in 2004 at the ripe old age of 101! We corresponded by mail when I saw a television story on his life on CNN one night.)

Preparations for a wedding and plans for the move to a new state made for a very hectic time. My mother threw a formal bridal shower, so selecting invitations for both a shower and a wedding kept us pretty busy. Dad and I drove to Williamsburg, Virginia to find a place to live. Dad would be starting his new teaching job at the College of William and Mary. We bought some furniture at my father's friend's store for our little "house" that we would rent in Williamsburg (actually it was more of a cottage!).

And then of course came the planning for our wedding. Seven weeks did not give us much time. Luckily, friend Doris Colantino loaned me her wedding gown that was quite beautiful and fit perfectly! Another friend, Jeanette Meltzer loaned me her bridal veil and together, the two were lovely. My brother Don flew in from Germany where he had been stationed during his army duty and Carol, Dad's sister came in from Georgia. Rabbi Leon Jick of Boston's Reform Temple Israel married us. We had met with Rabbi Jick prior to our wedding and were moved by his warmth and understanding and insight on many issues. He recently passed away…a great loss for so many. An Orthodox Cantor presided over our ceremony to honor my *Bubbe* Kamsky's more Orthodox traditions. Our wedding was a happy time for all. (See photos in Photo Section.)

```
____/_Y_/_
   __/___/__
   /   /
```

Chapter Twenty-One
SOME CLOSING REMARKS

So dear children and grandchildren and other readers: there you have it—my family history and childhood roots through food, culture and language. My story ends in 1955 when Dad and I married. I have enjoyed writing my tale and I hope you have enjoyed reading it. My journey has been a good one and I have tried to be candid. Of course, there is a lot more to tell about my life after leaving my parents' home—that might be Part II at another time.

As I have pointed out, family rituals, food and language of our ancestors link us to the past and to the future as well. And so today when I hear you, my children sigh *oy gevalt* (a humorous expression said when tired or frustrated), I smile to myself, knowing your grandparents would so enjoy hearing this. Thus, although Yiddish as a spoken language is disappearing, the love and humor of the language remains alive. Yiddish has left its mark upon our culture and upon our lives and hopefully, our grandkids too will remember to savor a word or expression.

The traditions and the culture of Judaism remain strong and vital as well. But as is the case with many people, some rituals that I practice today are different from those of my parents and grandparents. As a child and then a teenager I followed a path that was prescribed. As an adult, I began to think of why and how I practiced my Judaism. My own view of religion actually resides in the heart—by this I mean how we treat others, share and care and respect others—and support causes that promote peace—these are the things that matter to me. And Jewish people have been prominent players in the struggle for civil rights for all racial and religious groups.

Today America is a culture of great diversity that enriches and enhances our lives. Tradition also enriches our life experiences and helps us connect with the past. And tradition links us to the future. But our world is large and wide and we must remember to share our wealth, our wisdom and our resources.

And so as we enjoy our abundant food, let us remember the things important to all of us—family, good health, community and social responsibility, in our own families—and around the world as well. Protect and cherish our environment—as my son-in-law, Brian so often reminds us.

So to you grandkids, Sam, Max, Jake, Joey and Rachel and other young readers: As you go forward in life, there will be obstacles and disappointments—but you will overcome them and come away the stronger for it. Value education and curiosity and be of good humor. Remember to promote peace and kindness everywhere you go! Cheer for social justice. Show an interest in those outside your world. Invite a child sitting alone to join you at lunch. Talk to this new friend who may speak a different language but who wants to become your friend. Invite him or her to hang out with you and your pals. Be a peacemaker around your friends and family—and you will see and share in the delights and rewards.

We live in a world where new technology changes our lives almost daily. How we are able to fit an entire encyclopedia onto a tiny CD is pretty amazing. But let's not lose sight of what really matters to us and try to apply this same energy and our resources as well to work for solutions to the great problems of our country and our world: hunger, poverty, our environment and an end to wars.

We have the tools. Let's put them to work to make a safer, cleaner, healthier world for all. Maybe one day one of you grandkids will write your own family history. This book can be a starter for you. May you all have a great journey into the future!

May 2006

Artwork by Harriet M. Reiss

FAMILY RECIPE INDEX

"Food is the Most Primitive Form of Comfort"

—Sheila Graham, Singer and Actor

(The recipes that have an asterisk after them are the author's recipes.)

SOUPS:

FROM LENTIL SOUP
TO CABBAGE BORSCHT

MOM'S LENTIL SOUP*

2 meaty beef bones or 2 shoulder lamb chops
2 large onions, chopped
2 large garlic cloves, crushed
1 cup sliced celery with leaves
2-3 cups sliced carrots
1 green pepper, cut-up
1 lb. lentils, sorted and washed
2 cups cooked tomatoes, diced or stewed
1 ½ tsp salt
2 bay leaves
1 tsp thyme
1 tsp sage
3 cups water
3 cups chicken broth
1 package frozen chopped spinach, thawed

Brown meat bones in small amount of olive oil. Add onions and garlic and cook slightly. Add celery, green pepper and mix together. Then add rest of ingredients, except chopped spinach and mix well. Cook over low heat 1 ½ to 2 hours stirring every so often. If too thick, add more broth. Add spinach 15 minutes before end. Adjust seasonings. Take about two cups of soup and put through blender until lightly blended—add to soup for thickening. Cut up meat from bones into bite-sized pieces, being careful not to add gristle or fat and toss bones. If too thick, add chicken broth for desired consistency. Serves about 6-8 people.

CHICKEN SOUP

**My mother called this "Jewish penicillin" and felt,
like many others, that its soothing and nourishing broth
could help cure the common cold.**

4 lbs skinned, boned chicken parts (I use 3/4 thighs and ¼ breasts for
　　soup)
2 whole onions
3 or 4 carrots, scraped and cut into 2 inch lengths
4 ribs celery including tops
2 bay leaves
1 ½ - 2 tsp salt
¼ tsp or less white pepper
½ tsp dried thyme, optional
Water to cover

Clean and rinse chicken, cutting off fat and place in large pot with remaining ingredients. Bring to a boil, skimming off all foam. Cover and simmer for 1½ hours until chicken is tender. Remove chicken and carrots and few celery pieces and strain soup. Return vegetables to soup. Chill soup for several hours or overnight until soup forms gelatin-like consistency on top (it is fat). Remove this fat. Heat soup and serve. Keeps in refrigerator several days. Serves about six people.

COLD *SHAV*
(Russian for Sorrel or Sour Grass Soup)

This is a spinach-like vegetable cooked with other ingredients and served cold. Spinach can be used in place of *shav*. I do not have my mother's recipe; this was one of many recipes in my mother's head but never written down. The following recipe is similar.

1 lb *shav* (sour grass) or spinach
3 cups water
1 cup milk
Juice of one lemon
1 tsp salt
2 tablespoons sugar
1 egg, pasteurized
1 cucumber, peeled and sliced
Sour cream

Pick over and wash *shav* or spinach in cold water until clean. Drain and chop or cut fine. Cook in water with ½ tsp salt for about 10 minutes. Remove from burner and let cool. Beat egg with about ¼ cup of water, remaining ½ tsp of salt and 1 cup milk and pour slowly into partially cooled soup, stirring constantly. Refrigerate. To serve, top with cold sliced cucumbers and dollop of sour cream.

HOT BEET BORSCHT

**My mother never wrote down a recipe for Beet Borscht.
This one looks similar to what she cooked.**

1 bunch beets (about 3 bulbs)
1 lb meat and several bones
1 or 2 carrots, scraped and sliced
1 whole onion
2 tsp salt
4 cups water
1 tablespoon or more of sugar
Juice of one lemon

Place meat and bones in pot with water and bring to boil. Remove foam. Add onion, carrots, salt and sugar. Cover and simmer one hour. While meat is cooking, wash beets thoroughly and parboil. Remove skins and grate on coarse grater; then add grated beets to soup and cook slowly until meat is tender. Add lemon juice. Seasonings can be adjusted to taste. Serves about 4-6 people.

CABBAGE BORSCHT

**I do not have a recipe for my mother's borscht.
This one is similar but adds raisins. It is good.**

2 cups onions, chopped
½ cup celery, chopped
1 green pepper, coarsely chopped
2 lbs stew meat, optional or 1 large beefy soup bone
3-4 tablespoons olive oil
2 lbs cabbage, chopped
12 cups water
1 cup carrots, sliced
½ cup raisins, optional
2 tsp salt
1 tsp dill
Juice of 2 lemons
½ cup honey
¼ cup brown sugar
1 tsp pepper
1 (28 oz) can tomatoes, coarsely chopped

In large pot, sauté onions, celery, green pepper and beef bone or stew meat until meat or meat bone is browned and onions are tender. Add remaining ingredients, mix well and simmer 1-2 hours. Correct seasonings. Remove meat from bone and toss bone. Soup should have a rich sweet and sour taste. Serve with crusty bread. Freezes well. Serves about eight people.

FORSHPEIZ (APPETIZERS):

FROM CHOPPED LIVER
TO *GRIBBENES*

MOM'S CHOPPED LIVER*

1 lb fresh chicken livers (may also use beef liver for chunkier liver
    results)
2 cups chopped onions
3 or 4 tablespoons olive oil or margarine (my mother used chicken fat)
3 hard-boiled eggs
Salt and pepper to taste
1 or 2 tablespoons chicken broth, if needed

Wash chicken livers and remove fat and stringy parts. Drain. Broil
or sauté livers in a small amount of oil, turning to brown both sides and
cook until done scraping any livers pieces stuck to pan. Remove livers
with slotted spoon and cool a bit. Sauté onions in clean pan with
remaining oil until browned, adding small amount of extra oil if
necessary. Set aside to cool slightly. Using grinder or food processor,
blend liver, onions and hard-boiled eggs together. Watch carefully so
as to not over blend liver. Add salt and pepper and other seasonings as
you wish. If a chunkier chopped liver is desired, blend only slightly.
Food processors mash pretty quickly so this needs watching. (My
mother broiled beef liver and used a grinder and the consistency was
always chunkier.) A tablespoon of chicken broth can be added for
smoother consistency.

GRIBBENES

My mother made *gribbenes* fairly often; David especially loved it as a child although it's unhealthy because chicken fat is loaded with cholesterol—but I include it here for posterity and for the occasional *nosh*.

This recipe renders *schmaltz* (chicken fat) that means one cooks down the fat and some of the chicken skins and adds *tzibbeles* (onions) for extra flavor. The crisp fat and onions are mighty tasty. The liquid fat is then placed in the refrigerator and stored for cooking, e.g., it can be added to kasha instead of butter or to onions sautéed for chopped liver. Some kosher grocery stores still sell *schmaltz*. (After we got refrigeration and a tiny freezer in our Dorchester flat, my mother would save up and freeze the chicken fat from several chickens over a period of a few weeks. Then she'd have enough fat to prepare this recipe.) *Schmaltz* does add great flavor to foods but again, beware of its cholesterol and fat. Here's the simple recipe.

Remove fat from chicken and a few chicken skins, cutting both into bite-sized pieces. Cook fatty pieces and skins over low to moderate heat watching carefully because fat can splatter. After a few minutes, add one large coarsely chopped onion and stir until fat and onion pieces are crisp and brown. Drain on paper towels. Pass around as a *nosh* (snack) with challah or other bread. Can also be used as topping on baked potato.

SPICY FRESH HORSERADISH
FORSHPEIZ (APPETIZER)

This is a *forshpeiz* that Grandma Eisman often made on a Sunday.

1 fresh horseradish, shredded
½ red onion, grated
1 tablespoon *schmaltz* (chicken fat)
Salt and pepper to taste
1 tablespoon chicken broth, if desired or necessary to moisten mixture
1 fresh cucumber, peeled and chopped

Mix all ingredients, except cucumber, together until well blended. Refrigerate until cool. Divide into portions. Top each portion with chopped cucumber, lightly salted. Serves about 4 people.

SIDE DISHES:

FROM *KUGEL* TO *KASHE* AND *VARNISHKES*

GRANDMA EISMAN'S *LOKCHEN* *KUGEL* (Noodle Pudding)

½ lb medium noodles, cooked in salted water
3 eggs, beaten
1 cup sour cream
½ cup milk
1 lb cottage cheese
1 tsp vanilla
¼ cup sugar or less
salt and pepper to taste
1/8 lb margarine, melted
½ cup crushed cornflakes

Cook noodles in salted water and drain. Preheat oven to 375 degrees. Mix all ingredients except last two and stir until well blended. Add salt and pepper to taste. Pour into 9x9 greased baking dish. Mix melted margarine and cornflake topping and spread over kugel. If sweet topping is desired, add ½ cup brown sugar with the melted butter and crushed cornflakes and spread on top of kugel before baking. Bake in 375 degree oven for 1 hour. Serves about 4-6 people.

BUTTERMILK *KUGEL* (Pudding)

This is Chelle Rudick's recipe and the one that I make frequently.

1 lb large flat noodles cooked in salted water
4 eggs
1 quart buttermilk
½ cup sugar
¼ tsp salt
¼ lb butter, melted
1 cup golden raisins, optional

Topping
¾ cup brown sugar
¾ cup cornflake crumbs
1/8 lb melted butter to hold sugar and crumbs together

Cook and drain noodles. Preheat oven to 350 degrees. Add melted butter to milk. Add other ingredients, ending with raisins, if using. Pour into greased 9 x 12 pan. Bake at 350 for 45 minutes. Remove from oven. Sprinkle on topping. Return to oven and bake for 30 more minutes at 350. Serves about 8-10 people. Freezes well. Reheat thawed and almost room temperature kugel at 350 for 15-20 minutes or until heated through.

MOM'S *KASHE**

My mother used medium grain groats (I use whole when I can get it) and she added chicken fat in place of broth and butter. This is a very nourishing side dish that can be served in place of potatoes or rice and is Dad's favorite food. Bulk organic buckwheat groats are the best and available at Whole Foods markets.

1 cup buckwheat kasha (groats)—whole grain is best
1 egg
2 cups chicken broth
2 tablespoons or more of butter or margarine (Grandma Eisman used chicken fat)
¼ tsp salt or more
1/8 tsp pepper

Preheat oven to 325 degrees. Place groats in frying pan. Add beaten egg to kasha (groats) and stir till blended, cooking over very low flame until kasha grains are dry and separated. Pour into large saucepan, add 2 cups chicken broth and let simmer, stirring often, until all liquid is gone. Watch carefully—it only takes a few minutes although with whole groats, cooking time is longer. Add butter or margarine, salt and pepper. Transfer to ovenproof casserole dish and place in oven at 325. Bake about 20 minutes, stirring frequently. Add more butter, margarine or broth for desired consistency. Serve right away or cover and place on very low heat until serving. Serves 4-5 people.

MOM'S *KASHE* AND *VARNISHKES**

Follow the recipe for kasha shown on previous page, doubling recipe. Before placing in oven, assemble the following ingredients:

3 large onions, finely chopped
1 or 2 cups fresh mushrooms, finely chopped
1 lb bow tie noodles, cooked and drained according to directions
Salt and pepper to taste

Preheat oven to 325 degrees. Sauté onions in vegetable or olive oil until lightly browned; add chopped mushrooms and sauté for 5-10 minutes. Combine kasha, bow tie noodles with onion and mushrooms and 1 or 2 tablespoons chicken broth plus salt and pepper to taste. Stir until well blended. Pour into deep casserole dish, cover and bake at 325 for 20-25 minutes. Stir well. Uncover and bake 5 or 10 minutes longer. Serves about eight people.

AUNTIE ROSE'S *KASHE KNISHES*

1 cup lukewarm water
2 tsp sugar
1 package yeast
3 ½ cups flour
½ cup oil
1 egg
2 cups cooked kasha
6 large chopped onions

Place yeast and 2 tsp sugar into warm water. Add other ingredients except kasha and onions. Knead 5-10 minutes. Cover dough and let rise 10 minutes. Meantime chop and sauté 6 large onions until lightly browned and add to kasha. Preheat oven to 350 degrees. Take 12 chunks of dough and roll into 24 flat pieces. Add large spoonful of kasha and onion mixture onto each piece of dough, pinching edges together and using flour if necessary for ease in closing knish. Place on greased tin and bake for 20-25 minutes at 350 on middle rack. Makes about 24 knishes.

MEAT OR LIVER *KNISHES*

My mother did not have a recipe for knishes; this is one version. (In place of chicken fat in recipe, experiment with different seasonings in the filling.)

Dough
2 tsp baking powder
2 cups flour
½ cup oil
2 eggs, well beaten
½ cup water

Sift dry ingredients together; add oil, eggs and water, blending all ingredients until it forms dough. Knead well. Divide dough in half and roll out thin on floured board. Cut into small squares or circles.

Filling
1 lb liver, broiled and ground—or 1 lb meat, cooked and ground
2 garlic cloves, mashed
3 medium onions, chopped
2 carrots, finely chopped, optional
¾ tablespoon chicken fat or olive oil
1 tsp salt
1/8 tsp pepper

Preheat oven to 375 degrees. Saute onions and garlic in chicken fat or oil and add to remaining ingredients. Place small amount of meat or liver mixture onto each square or circle and pinch together using fingers or fork dipped in flour. Brush with oil and bake at 375 for about 25 minutes. Or beat one egg lightly with one tsp cold water and brush knishes before baking—this makes for a brown and shiny crust. Serve warm.

GRANDMA EISMAN'S CHEESE BLINTZES

Dough
3 eggs
1 cup water with ½ cup milk, mixed
1 ½ cups flour
1 ½ tsp salt

Mix dough ingredients well and put through strainer. Heat tiny amount of margarine in small frying pan—my mother used paper napkin smeared with tiny amount of margarine with which she greased frying pan between crepes. Pour about 3 tablespoons batter into greased hot frying pan. Rotate pan so batter covers bottom and some of the sides as well. Lay each cooked crepe onto clean dishtowel. (My mother always used a wooden board under the dishtowel and she'd slam to loosen each cooked crepe from pan onto the board. I remember the slamming sound.)

Filling
1 - 1½ lbs Cottage cheese or Farmers' cheese
2 eggs
1-2 tablespoons sugar to taste
Margarine and oil for frying

Mix filling ingredients well. Place large spoonful of filling on the browned side of the crepe, fold over once, tuck ends in and fold again. Place blintzes into frying pan with seam side down and brown in mix of margarine and oil, turning to brown both sides. Serve with sour cream and jelly.

CUPCAKE BLINTZES

Tastes like blintzes without the work.
Do not use low fat dairy products for this recipe.

1 lb small curd cottage cheese
3-4 tablespoons sour cream
3 eggs
1 tsp vanilla
½ cup Bisquick mix
3 tablespoons sugar
½ cup butter, softened or ½ cup margarine, softened (do not use
    low-fat margarine)

Preheat oven to 350 degrees. Again, do not use low-fat dairy products for this recipe. You need the fat for ease in removing muffins from pan. Beat ingredients together until fairly smooth. Pour into well-greased muffin tins (use Pam or butter) about ¾ full. Bake at 350 degrees for 35-40 minutes until lightly browned. Cool before removing from tins. Serve with sour cream and/or jelly.

STEWED CABBAGE

This is a great sweet and sour flavor.

1 medium head cabbage
1 large onion, chopped
1 or 2 celery stalks, sliced diagonally
2 tablespoons olive oil
1 cup sliced carrots, optional
1 tsp salt
¼ tsp pepper
1/3-cup brown sugar
1 (8 oz) can tomato sauce
¼ cup water
1/3 cup raisins (I use golden raisins)
1 or 2 medium cut up tomatoes

Cut cabbage into quarters, and then slice into chunky pieces. Set aside. Sauté onions, celery and carrots in olive oil until onions are transparent. Add cabbage and remaining ingredients except raisins and bring to boil. Simmer in covered pot for about 45 minutes, adding raisins in last 10-15 minutes of cooking. Serves 6-8 people.

MOM'S POTATO *LATKES**

15-16 medium potatoes (I mix red and white potatoes)
3 medium onions cut into small quarters
1 or 2 large carrots, scraped and cut into 2 inch pieces
4 or 5 large eggs
¼ cup matzo meal (or bread crumbs if you don't have matzo meal)
2 tsp salt or more depending on your taste
Pinch of white pepper
Vegetable oil for frying

Peel potatoes if skin is course; otherwise scrub skins under water and let dry thoroughly (this is important). Cut potatoes into small chunks. Using food processor, grate vegetables, adding eggs, matzo meal (or breadcrumbs) and salt to mixture. Stir until well blended. Heat one inch or less of oil in frying pan and drop about one tablespoon mixture into oil, turning when nicely browned on bottom. When latkes are crisp, drain on paper towels. Continue cooking latkes on medium-high heat, adding more oil as needed to make them brown and crisp.

As you cook, stir uncooked mixture often to blend starch and juices. Cool cooked latkes a few minutes. Toss any leftover starch or juices…but if you stir mixture often while cooking, there usually isn't much liquid left. Latkes can be refrigerated until ready to serve by first placing them in a single layer on pan (use two if needed). Bring to room temperature and reheat at 350 degrees for about 10 minutes or until hot and crisp. (My mother used to grate by hand potatoes and onions. It was a tedious task but I never remember her complaining about it.) Makes about two dozen or more latkes.

Note: This recipe can also be used for potato kugel (pudding). To make the potato kugel, pour the batter into a large greased baking pan and bake at 325 degrees for about two hours. The top will be very crusty—kind of like one very large thick latke!)

HELSEL

Grandma Eisman made *helsel* often on a Friday night. *Helsel* is the skin from the neck of the chicken stuffed with breadcrumbs and seasoning and then roasted with the chicken and vegetables. She didn't have a recipe but the following would do it.

1/3 cup breadcrumbs
1 small grated onion, sautéed
½ tsp salt
Dash of pepper
1 tablespoon chicken fat or olive oil
Bit of water or chicken broth for moistening, if needed
1 egg (optional)

Cut skin neck off chicken or other bird. (I remember that my mother turned the neck inside out, scalded it in hot water to scrape off fat, and then turned the neck back to right side.) Mix together ingredients. Sew up wide end of neck and then stuff neck. Sew up other end. Roast with chicken or cook with Carrot Tzimmes and Meat.

KREPLACH

My mother did not have a recipe for *Kreplach*. I made this recipe a couple years ago. *Kreplach* is a popular Jewish appetizer.

Dough
1 cup flour
½ tsp salt
2 eggs

Beat eggs in bowl; add salt and flour gradually to make stiff dough, using more flour if necessary. Roll into thin sheet and cut into 2" squares.

Meat Mixture
¾ lb cooked meat (pot roast, cooked hamburger, etc.)
2 carrots, grated
1 onion, grated
½ tsp salt or more
Dash of pepper

Mix meat mixture with vegetables and seasonings. Place spoonful of mixture onto each 2" square. Fold dough over meat, forming a triangle and press edges together firmly using fork or fingers dipped in flour. Drop into boiling salted water or broth and boil about 10 minutes. Drain and add to chicken soup. Kreplach may also be sautéed in olive oil until lightly browned and served as an appetizer or side dish.

MAIN DISHES:

FROM CHANUKAH BRISKET
TO CHALUPTSES

MOM'S CHANUKAH BRISKET*

This is a recipe I have perfected over a few Chanukahs.

1 (5 lb) brisket or sirloin tip roast
3 crushed garlic cloves
5 large carrots, scraped and cut in 1" pieces
3 large onions cut in chunk pieces
1 or 2 green peppers, cut-up
½ tsp pepper
1 tsp paprika
1 tablespoon salt
2½ cups water
6 oz ketchup
¼ cup brown sugar

Preheat oven to 350 degrees. Place all ingredients except ketchup and brown sugar in large roasting pot. Cover and bake at 350 for about 1½ to 2 hours or until meat is soft enough to cut but not tender. Remove from oven, cool slightly and slice meat.

Add ketchup and brown sugar to vegetables and stir completely. Pour about 1/3 of mixture into large pitcher. Stir small batches in blender or food processor. Do not over-blend; mixture should be chunky. Return sliced meat to roasting pot, top with blended mixture and rest of unblended vegetables. Add a bit of chicken broth for desired consistency. At this point, roast can be refrigerated. When ready to serve dinner, cover roast and bake another 30 minutes at 350 degrees until tender.

BRISKET *TSIMMES*** WITH CARROTS AND SWEET POTATO

Usually cooked and served on Rosh Hashanah/Yom Kippur for a sweet year. The sugar amounts are correct. This is a sweet meat dish.

1 5 lb. Brisket
16 carrots, scraped
4 sweet potatoes, peeled and cut into chunks
3 onions, chopped
3 garlic cloves, mashed
2 tsp salt
½ tsp pepper
¼ tsp nutmeg
1 ½ cups brown sugar
¾ cup white sugar
4 cups boiling water
Cornstarch (about 1 tablespoon) mixed in cold water to thicken gravy

Preheat oven to 350 degrees. Brown brisket in small amount of olive oil on top of stove. Put in large roaster, and place carrots, sweet potatoes and onions around meat. Cover with 4 cups boiling water. Season meat with garlic and half the salt and pepper. Then season vegetables with remaining salt, pepper and nutmeg. Cover and cook for 2 hours at 350 degrees.

Remove from oven. Add both sugars, pouring sugar all over and under vegetables. Reduce heat to 300, cover and cook for 1½ hours longer. When ready to serve, remove meat and slice. Place sliced meat and vegetables in another pot. Strain about 2/3 of liquid and add cornstarch (mixed in very small amount of cold water) and simmer until desired thickened. Meantime, return sliced meat and vegetables and remaining liquid into roaster and cook for another 30 minutes at 300 until ready to serve. Pass thickened gravy.

**The word *tsimmes* also means "making a major issue out of a minor thing or fuss over nothing."

MOM'S *GUBLETS**

This recipe is basically Chicken Fricassee with Meat Balls but with some additions. The *Gublets* are cut-up *pupicks* (giblets) and in Jewish tradition, reserved for a favorite child. (I don't remember my mother telling us the "favorites" in children custom nor do I like such a custom but I mention it here after reading about it.) Grandma Eisman used a mix of ground chicken and ground beef for the balls that were added after stewing the chopped giblets and vegetables for a bit. She also left chicken skins and bones in for more flavor. My mother did not have a recipe—this is one I put together that works. When we lived in Dorchester, I remember that my mother added skinned and cleaned "chopped chicken feet" to this recipe! Remember— those chickens were kosher and thus got the full kosher treatment— soaking in cold water for ½ hour and then salting with kosher salt to draw out remaining blood, ending with several cold rinses.

Meat balls

2 lbs ground meat (mix of chicken and beef)

2 eggs

2 medium onions, grated

1 package Knorr's Dry Onion Mix

4 slices bread, soaked in cold water and squeezed to get excess water out—I actually use 2-3 tablespoons seasoned breadcrumbs and a bit of water to moisten entire mixture. (For Passover, substitute 2 tablespoons matzo meal for bread and a bit of broth for desired consistency.)

Salt and pepper to taste

Combine ingredients and shape into small balls.

(Continued next page)

Chicken and vegetable mixture

4 lbs skinless chicken parts (Grandma left skin and bones which
    does add flavor)
1 or 2 giblets or more, chopped
3 garlic cloves, minced
3 medium onions, diced
3 stalks celery, sliced
3 medium carrots, scraped and sliced
8 oz fresh mushrooms, sliced thick (optional)
1 tsp thyme
1 tsp marjoram
Salt and pepper to taste
3 cups chicken broth

In large pot slowly sauté onions and garlic in small amount of olive oil. Add giblets, celery, carrots and mushrooms (optional), salt and pepper. Push aside vegetables, add a bit more oil and sprinkle paprika into pot for browning chicken. Add chicken and sauté till brown. Add thyme and marjoram, stirring all seasonings together. Add soup stock and simmer for ten minutes. Add meatballs, cover and cook slowly for 1 ½ hours or until chicken and meatballs are cooked. Check every so often to be sure liquid is sufficient and food is not sticking to pot. Add more broth or water if needed. To thicken gravy, mix tablespoon or two of cornstarch in same amount cold water, stir well and add to gravy. Bring to light boil for a few minutes. Serve over rice or noodles.

CHOLENT

Cholent (Flanken or brisket with potatoes and lima beans) is a traditional Sabbath dish for Orthodox Jewish families who did not light the stove on the Sabbath. The brisket served the family after the synagogue service on Saturday. Just before lighting the Sabbath candles on Friday evening, the *Cholent* was placed in the oven at about 300 degrees and left there overnight so that upon returning from synagogue on Saturday after services, it was ready to serve. (Talk about slow cooking...this is it!) Although neither my mother nor I cooked this dish, I am including it here because it is traditional, especially among Orthodox Jews.

1 ½ lbs meat (flanken or brisket)
6 medium potatoes, peeled and cut in 1" slices
1 onion, chopped
1 cup or more dried lima beans
1 ½ tablespoon flour
1 tablespoon salt
Dash of pepper
1/8 tsp ginger
2 tablespoons chicken fat or other oil
Paprika

Preheat oven to 400 degrees. Grease bottom of deep, heavy pot with small amount of the fat. Lay beans on bottom and place meat over beans. Mix chopped onion with flour and seasoning. Place layer of potatoes on meat and sprinkle with some of the onion/flour mixture. Repeat with potato and onion mixture until both are used up. Drizzle with chicken fat or other oil onto meat and potato mixture and sprinkle with paprika. Add 1 ½ cups water, pouring it down into the side of the pot. Bring to boil on top of stove, cover tightly and place in a 400 degree oven for ½ hour. After half hour, turn heat low to maybe 275 degrees, keeping pot tightly covered and cook slowly overnight or all day until ready to serve.

ROAST TONGUE

This is a cow's cooked tongue recipe that my father loved and it actually tasted good; but when I think of cooking a cow's tongue now, it's not too tempting and I know Dad would never eat it! I would guess cow's tongue might still be sold at some kosher butchers. I don't have a recipe but it went something like this: Cook tongue until tender (I don't know how long—ask butcher. Soaking tongue for an hour or two before cooking might help tenderize tongue. Again, ask butcher.) Remove skin and slice tongue. Sauté 1 or 2 onions with some minced garlic until lightly browned and add a bit of salt and pepper. Add ½ cup of chicken broth or ½ cup of the tongue cooking water and stir together. Pour over sliced tongue and bake in oven at about 325 for maybe 20-30 minutes. That should do it.

STEWED LAMB NECK WITH VEGETABLES

**This was one of Grandma Eisman's favorite dishes;
I don't have a recipe so I'll ad lib here.**

About 2 lbs lamb shoulder, cut-up
1 or 2 garlic cloves, minced
1 or more large onions, chopped
1+ cup sliced celery and couple bunches of celery leaves
3-4 carrots, sliced
Salt and pepper to taste
Thyme and marjoram, about ½ teaspoon of each
½ cup dry red wine (white wine is ok too)
¾ cup water or chicken broth
4-5 red potatoes, peeled

Sauté onion and garlic in small amount of oil. Add lamb and brown.
Add celery and carrots and stir. Add seasonings to water or broth, add
wine and pour over meat and vegetables. Cover and bring to light boil.
Simmer one hour, stirring occasionally. Add extra liquid if needed.
Add peeled and cut-up (bite size) potatoes and cook for additional 15
minutes or less only until potatoes are tender but still have a bite. If
gravy is too thin, thicken by adding one tablespoon cornstarch in 2
tablespoons cold water and stir completely; then add to gravy. Bring to
boil for a few minutes. Dunking bread into gravy is good!

CHALUPTSES

Grandma Eisman made *Chaluptses* (Stuffed Cabbage) often. She did not have a recipe; this recipe is one I use and is good.

Prepare cabbage leaves

Put whole head of cabbage in hot simmering water for a few minutes until the leaves are soft enough to separate. Separate leaves and place on dishtowel. (Some cooks freeze whole cabbage for a couple days and then defrost. I tried this once and I prefer the hot water method.)

Sauce (I use one large pot for making sauce and cooking *Chaluptses*)

2 medium onions, chopped
2 garlic cloves, minced
1 28 oz can tomatoes, chopped
1 12 oz can tomato paste
1 cup ketchup (my mother used Campbell's tomato soup)
¾ cup brown sugar
½ tsp salt
½ to 1 cup sliced carrots, optional

Sauté chopped onions and garlic in small amount of olive oil until lightly cooked. Stir in remaining ingredients and blend together, cooking 3-4 minutes. Add sliced carrots if including. Remove from heat. Take two or more cups of the sauce and set aside. Prepare meat mixture.

(Continued next page)

Chaluptses (Continued)

Meat Mixture
2 lbs ground beef (can use 1 lb beef and 1 lb turkey)
2 eggs
1 large onion, chopped
1 tsp salt
¼ tsp pepper
3–4 tablespoons raw white rice, optional

Combine ground beef, eggs, onion, salt and pepper and rice, if using. Place ¼ cup meat mixture in the center of each leaf. Fold over once, tuck ends in and fold again, this time tightly. Place rolls carefully into sauce in pot with seam side down and pour remaining two cups of sauce over rolls. Cover and cook about 1 hour. Shake pan slightly every so often to be sure no food is sticking to bottom of pan. If more liquid is needed, add beef or chicken broth. Taste and adjust seasonings. This recipe can also be prepared in the oven at 350 for about 2 hours.

PASSOVER FOODS:

FROM *GEFILTE* FISH
TO VEGETABLE *KUGELA*

MOM'S *GEFILTE* FISH for PASSOVER*

**This recipe comes from years of watching and helping my
mother make her fish plus some of my own tricks. She actually
did not have a recipe but tasted the raw fish mixture a time or
two (she didn't swallow) to check for enough seasoning. I've
come up with this recipe. My mother vigorously chopped her
fish in a wooden bowl for 90 minutes until mixture was light and
fluffy which, she often said, was the key to making good fish.
(Every so often during the chopping, she took seconds of rest
and gave a deep sigh; later I was big enough to help.) We lucky
modern cooks can use our food processors.**

5-6 lbs whole fish (mix of whitefish, walleye, trout or pike) Have
butcher grind fish, saving fish bones and heads and some skins for your
cooking—this really adds to flavor.

4 tsp salt, divided
1½ tsp pepper, divided
4+ large onions, 2 sliced and 2 grated
4-5 carrots, sliced
2 celery sticks, sliced
1+ tsp sugar, optional
4 cups water
4 eggs
1 or 2 finely grated carrots, optional
½ cup water with 1 Knorr's fish cube dissolved
¼ cup matzo meal—or bread crumbs when not Passover

Rinse bones and heads of fish in cool water and place in the largest
pot you have—I use an 8 quart pot. Add 2 tsp of the salt and ¾ tsp
pepper, 1 tsp sugar, 2 sliced onions, carrots and celery. Add water,
bring to boil and simmer on low heat.

(Continued next page)

Put ground fish into wooden chopping bowl. Grate and add remaining two large onions, salt and pepper and grated carrots if desired. Dissolve Knorr's fish cube in ½ cup boiling water and cool. (I use ¼ cup boiling water, and then add ice to cool liquid down quickly.) Add to mixture, along with ¼ cup matzo meal. Chop and mix and blend by hand for 90 minutes, necessary for a light and fluffy texture, my mother often said. Today we modern cooks are lucky to have our food processors do the work for us. So chop and blend and whip fish mixture until light and fluffy. Form into balls, using 1/3 cup (or less for smaller balls). (My mother wrapped fish skins around some of her oval shaped balls. She'd also stuff the heads of fish and add them to the pot. Lastly, she sometimes added 2-3 peeled and cut-up small red potatoes—I don't; if you do, add more salt and seasoning to broth. Grandma Eisman also placed sliced onions in between layers of balls so they wouldn't stick. I don't—it's not necessary and only makes indentations in the balls. But I mention it here to honor all that my mother did to make her gefilte fish look and taste so great!)

Okay…drop balls gently into boiling fish broth and cook covered for about 1½ hours. Baste every so often and shake pan slightly to avoid fish sticking to bottom. After cooking remove balls carefully onto two large platters. Decorate with cooked carrot slices. Remove all bones and heads and toss. Strain vegetables and remaining juices and pour over fish balls. Chill. Best if made 2 or 3 days before eating so seasonings can blend. Makes about 20-22 balls.

MATZO BALLS (*Knaedlach* in Yiddish)

This is the recipe on the Streit's box of matzo meal and is the best matzo ball recipe. I used to separate yolks and whites and the result was not as good as this recipe. My father, Sam Eisman, always said Streit's Matzo was the best.

1 cup matzo meal
½ cup water
4 beaten eggs
1/3 cup melted shortening (I use olive, canola or peanut oil—I think canola is best here)
1 tsp salt
Dash of pepper

Add water, melted shortening, salt and pepper to the beaten eggs. Mix well. Add matzo meal and stir thoroughly. Refrigerate one hour. Form into balls and drop into 1½ quarts boiling water to which one tablespoon salt has been added. Cook 20 minutes. Makes about 12 matzo balls.

PASSOVER SPINACH SOUFFLE

½ cup chopped onion
½ cup chopped carrots
1 large clove garlic, minced
1 tablespoon butter or margarine, melted, or 1 tablespoon olive oil
1 package (8 oz) cream cheese, softened
8 oz farmer's cheese
1/8 tsp each salt and pepper
3 eggs
2 packages (10 oz) frozen chopped spinach, thawed and well drained
¼ tsp paprika
1/8 tsp ground nutmeg

Preheat oven to 325 degrees. Cook onion and carrots in butter or olive oil until tender. Beat cream cheese, farmer cheese, salt and pepper with electric mixer until well blended. Add onion and carrot mixture. Beat in eggs, one at a time, mixing well after each one. Blend in spinach. Pour mixture into greased 9-inch square baking pan. Sprinkle with nutmeg and paprika and cover. Bake at 325 degrees for 30 minutes; uncover. Bake an additional 15 minutes. Makes 8 servings.

PASSOVER ONION KUGEL

6 eggs, separated
2 cups finely chopped onions
½ cup chopped carrots, optional
1/3 cup peanut oil
1/3 cup matzo meal
1½ tsp salt
¼ tsp pepper

Preheat oven to 350 degrees. Beat egg yolks until thick and creamy. Add onion and carrots, oil, matzo meal, salt and pepper. Mix well. In separate bowl beat egg whites until stiff and fold into onion mixture. Pour into buttered 2-quart casserole. Bake at 350 for 30 minutes or until knife inserted into center comes out clean. To heat cooked kugel, bring to room temperature and bake at 350 for 15-20 minutes.

GRANDMA EISMAN'S PASSOVER *KUGELAH* (Small Kugels)

This recipe uses *farfel* (chopped matzo) that is available at Passover time in most stores.

4 eggs
3 cups *farfel*
4 eggs, separated
salt and pepper to taste

Preheat oven to 400 degrees. Cover *farfel* with hot water. Drain. Pour cold water over *farfel* and drain. Beat egg yolks and add to *farfel* mixture. Add salt and pepper. Beat egg whites and carefully add to farfel until well blended. Pour into well-greased muffin tins and bake at 400 degrees for about 45 minutes.

INDIVIDUAL PASSOVER VEGETABLE KUGELA (Small Kugels)

6 tablespoons unsalted butter
1 or 2 minced garlic cloves
¼ chopped green pepper
1 cup chopped onion
½ cup chopped celery
½ cup grated carrots
1 (10 oz) package frozen chopped spinach
3 eggs, beaten
1 ½ tsp salt
1/8 tsp pepper
¾ cup matzo meal
½ tsp each thyme and sage
1-2 tablespoons or more of chicken broth, if desired

Preheat oven to 350 degrees. Sauté green pepper, onion, celery, carrots and garlic in butter for about 5 minutes. Cook spinach and drain. Combine all vegetables. Add eggs, salt, pepper, thyme, sage and matzo meal and stir until well blended, adding chicken broth by tablespoon until desired consistency. Spoon into well-greased muffin tins. Bake at 350 for 40-45 minutes or until firm and lightly browned on top. Allow to sit for 10 minutes before removing and serving. Makes 24 kugela. (I generally make these kugela in the mini-muffin pans (grandkids like this size) and bake at 350 for 30-35 minutes until done.)

AUNTIE ROSE'S PASSOVER ROLLS

2 cups water
1 tsp salt
1 tablespoon sugar
½ cup oil
2 cups matzo meal
5 eggs

Boil together water, salt, sugar and oil. Let cool. Put in *shisel* (pan) with 2 cups matzo meal. Let cool. Add eggs, one at a time, mixing well. Shape into rolls and bake on a lightly greased cookie tin at 375 for about 20 minutes.

FRIED MATZO

2-3 matzos
3-4 eggs
Hot water
Salt to taste
Pinch or more of pepper
Other seasonings of your choice

Break matzos into small/medium-sized pieces. Add hot water to moisten matzos; then drain. Beat eggs with salt and pepper, other seasonings and add to matzo pieces. Fry in margarine/olive oil chopping pieces and turning so all the matzo pieces get brown and crisp. Adding more margarine or olive oil and turning up heat helps in getting matzo brown and crispy. Serve with applesauce and sour cream.

MATZO MEAL *LATKES*
(Joel Reiss's favorite)

½ cup matzo meal
¾ tsp salt
1 tablespoon sugar
¾ cup cold water
3 eggs
Peanut or canola oil for frying

Combine matzo meal, salt and sugar. Separate eggs. Beat yolks slightly and combine with water. Add liquids to the dry ingredients. Cover and place in refrigerator for 30 minutes. Beat egg whites until stiff. Fold egg whites into the matzo mixture. Drop by tablespoon onto hot greased pan, adding oil as necessary to fry latkes. Brown latkes on both sides. Drain on paper towels.

HOLIDAY DESSERTS:

FROM FLOURLESS CHOCOLATE CAKE TO *TAIGLACH*

MOM'S FLOURLESS CHOCOLATE CAKE #1*

4 oz bittersweet (not unsweetened) chocolate
1 tsp vanilla
1 tablespoon espresso or very strong coffee
1 tablespoon brandy
6 tablespoons butter
½ cup sugar
½ cup ground almonds
3 large eggs

Preheat oven to 300 degrees. In heavy saucepan, melt 4 oz chocolate over low heat. Add vanilla, coffee and brandy. Add butter, sugar and ground almonds. Heat until well blended and remove from heat. Beat 3 large egg yolks until lemon colored and stir them into the chocolate mixture. Whip 3 large egg whites until stiff and carefully fold them into chocolate mixture. Pour batter into a buttered 8-inch springform cake pan. Bake at 300 degrees for 45 minutes. The cake will have some cracks on top and a tester will not come out clean. Let cake cool completely on a rack and then remove the side of the pan. Top each serving with a generous dollop of whipped cream. Serves about 8-10 people.

MOM'S FLOURLESS CHOCOLATE CAKE #2*

6 tablespoons unsalted butter, plus more for pan
1½ cups semisweet chocolate chips (or 8 oz chopped bittersweet chocolate)
6 eggs, separated
½ cup granulated sugar
Powdered sugar for garnish

Preheat oven to 275 degrees. Butter bottom and sides of a 9-inch springform cake pan. Place butter and chocolate in a large bowl and microwave in 30-second increments, stirring each time, until melted; cool slightly. Whisk in egg yolks. In another bowl, beat egg whites to soft peaks. Gradually add sugar and beat until egg whites are stiff and glossy. Whisk ¼ of whites into chocolate mixture; then gently fold mixture into remaining whites. Pour batter into prepared pan and smooth top. Bake at 275 degrees for 45-50 minutes or until cake pulls away from sides of pan and is just set in center. Cool completely on a wire rack. Dust with powdered sugar and serve.

PASSOVER CHOCOLATE MERINGUE PIE

The meringue in this pie is firm and serves as the crust for the pie.

4 egg whites
¾ cups sugar
1 cup ground pecans
1 pint whipped cream
4 squares sweetened or semi-sweet baking chocolate
2 tablespoons sugar

Preheat oven to 300 degrees. Beat egg whites until foamy, gradually adding sugar. Continue beating until stiff peaks form. Gently fold in nuts and turn into greased and floured 10" pie plate. Bake in 300 degrees oven for approximately one hour. Meanwhile beat 1 pint (16 oz) whipping cream, adding 2 tablespoons sugar. Melt 3 squares chocolate and fold into cream. Pour into cooled pie shell. Shave remaining chocolate over filling and decorate with pecan halves, if desired.

JOEL NELSON'S CARMEL MATZOS CRUNCH

4-6 unsalted matzos
1 cup (2 sticks) unsalted butter or unsalted Passover margarine
1 cup packed brown sugar
¾ cup coarsely chopped semisweet chocolate chips or semi sweet chocolate
1 cup toasted slivered almonds (optional)

Line a large (or 2 small) cookie sheet(s) completely with foil. Cover foil sheet with baking parchment. This is very important since mixture becomes sticky during baking. Line bottom of cookie sheet evenly with matzos, cutting extra pieces, as required, fitting any spaces. In a 3-quart heavy-bottomed saucepan, combine butter and brown sugar. Cook over medium heat, stirring constantly, until mixture comes to a boil (about 2 to 4 minutes). Boil 3 minutes, stirring constantly. Remove from heat and pour over matzos, covering completely.

Place cookie sheet in preheated 375-degree oven and immediately reduce oven temperature to 350 degrees. Bake 15 minutes, checking every few minutes to make sure mixture is not burning (if it seems to be browning too quickly, remove pan from oven, reduce temperature to 325 degrees and replace pan). Remove from oven and sprinkle immediately with chocolate. Let stand 5 minutes; then spread melted chocolate over matzos. While still warm, sprinkly toasted almonds on chocolate and break into squares or odd shapes. Chill, still in pan, in freezer until set.

HAMANTASHEN FOR PURIM

**This is a triangular pocket of dough with filling, baked and
eaten as dessert during Purim that celebrates the defeat of
Haman, who wanted to destroy all Jews in Persia (now Iran).
Haman wore a triangular shaped hat—thus the shape of
*Hamentashen.***

¼ lb butter
½ cup of sugar
3 eggs
½ tsp vanilla
juice and rind of one orange
2 cups of flour
1 tsp baking powder
Solo fillings *mohn* (poppy seeds) or finely chopped apples

Preheat oven to 375 degrees. Cream butter and sugar. Add three
eggs, ½ tsp vanilla and juice and rind of one orange and beat well. Then
add flour and baking powder and beat again. Chill overnight.

Roll mixture out onto floured surface (keeping rolling pin in some
flour) and cut into 3" circles with a floured glass. Fill with small
amount of Solo *mohn* (poppy seed) or peeled, chopped and seasoned
fresh apple or other fruit. (Grandma Eisman didn't use canned mohn.
She cooked raw *mohn.*) Fold up, pinching edges, using fork dipped in
flour and shape into triangular shape. Brush with egg diluted with 1 tsp
cold water. Bake on a greased pan at 375 until brown (about 10-15
minutes)

Note: My mother used to make *hamantashen* but she never used a
recipe. Her *hamantashen* were huge and nicely browned. I never cared
for the prune filling nor the *mohn.* The recipe here is one I have used a
few times in the past using a filling of chopped apples or other fruit, and
it is good.

CHANUKAH COOKIES

½ cup vegetable shortening
½ cup brown sugar
½ cup white sugar
2 eggs
1 tsp vanilla
1 or 2 tablespoons orange juice
2½ cups flour
2 tsp baking powder
½ tsp salt
Colored sugars

Preheat oven to 400 degrees. Cream shortening and sugars and beat in eggs. Add vanilla and orange juice and mix well. Mix flour, baking powder and salt and blend into shortening mixture until smooth. Divide dough into 2 or 3 portions. Refrigerate for at least one hour. On floured surface, roll out each dough portion to ¼" thickness. Cut out with Chanukah cookie cutters dipped in flour. Sprinkle with colored sugars. Re-roll scraps and continue cutting out until all dough is used. Bake cookies on ungreased cookie tin at 400 degrees for about 10 minutes or until lightly browned.

MOM'S TRADITIONAL HONEY CAKE*

½ cup cooking oil, either peanut or canola
1 cup sugar
3 eggs
1 cup honey
1 cup strong cold coffee (2 tsp instant is ok)
3 cups flour
2 tsp baking powder
1 tsp baking soda
½ tsp cloves
½ tsp nutmeg
½ tsp allspice
½ tsp cinnamon
½ tsp ginger
¼ tsp salt
raisins and nuts, optional

Preheat oven to 350 degrees. Blend cooking oil and sugar; add eggs and blend well. Add remaining ingredients, mixing well. If adding raisins or nuts, stir lightly into batter. Pour into greased tube pan and bake at 350 degrees for 45 minutes. (Nuts of your choice may also be sprinkled onto top of batter, pressing lightly into batter before baking.) Check for doneness by inserting toothpick into batter; if it comes out clean, cake is done.

CHOCOLATE HONEY CAKE

This is my newest honey cake recipe that you all like.

2 ¾ cups flour
½ cup cocoa
1 tablespoon baking powder
¾ tsp baking soda
½ tsp salt
1 ½ tsp cinnamon
½ tsp cloves
1 cup corn or peanut oil
1 cup honey
1 cup white sugar
½ cup brown sugar, packed
4 eggs
2 tsp vanilla
1 cup strong brewed coffee
½ cup coarsely chopped semi-sweet chocolate, optional
1/3 cup slivered almonds, optional

Preheat oven to 350 degrees. Generously spray with Pam a nine or ten inch tube or angel food cake pan. In large bowl, whisk together flour, cocoa, baking powder, baking soda, salt, cinnamon and cloves. In second bowl, beat and blend oil, honey, white and brown sugars and blend well. Add eggs, vanilla and coffee and blend again. Fold in dry ingredients and blend about 2 minutes until smooth. Fold in chocolate chips if using. Pour batter into prepared cake pan; sprinkle with almonds if using. Bake about 60-75 minutes in 350-degree oven until cake springs back when gently pressed with fingertips. Cool before removing from pan. Serve with generous dollop of whipped cream.

MARCIA HINITZ' MOM'S *TAIGLACH*

This dessert is generally made for Rosh Hashanah and Yom Kippur for a sweet New Year. *Taiglach* are small pieces of dough baked and then simmered in honey. The small dough pieces are also called *Mandlen* in this recipe. You all liked my last batch. I've tried other *Taiglach* recipes—but this one is the best. (Also this recipe gives you another option to build a pyramid with *Taiglach* pieces.)

Dough
3 eggs, well beaten
Scant ¼ cup oil (I use Canola)
1 tsp baking powder
1/8 cup sugar
2 ½ cups flour
¼ tsp salt
¼ teaspoon ginger

Preheat oven to 375. Mix eggs and oil together and add other ingredients. Knead for few minutes, cover with plastic wrap and let rest 5-10 minutes. Roll pencil-thin between floured palms and place onto ungreased cookie sheet. Cut into tiny pieces, about ½ inch each. Heat oven to 350 degree. Bake 18-20 minutes until golden brown and puffy. While *taiglach* are in oven, wet wooden board with brandy, cognac or whiskey and sprinkle chopped walnuts on it in preparation for dipping *taiglach* after they have been cooked in honey mixture. Syrup recipe for *taiglach* follows on next page.

(Continued next page)

Syrup
1 lb honey
½ cup sugar
1 tsp ginger
Walnuts and golden raisins, optional

Bring syrup to rolling boil. Add *taiglach* or *mandlen* (baked bits) and simmer approximately 15-20 minutes or until desired shade of light brown. Just before removing *mandlen,* add walnuts and golden raisins to mixture, coat well and then remove the *mandlen,* nuts and raisins to plate and form a pyramid. Or if you choose other method, dip slightly cooled honey-coated *mandlen* pieces into brandy/walnut mixture, coating each piece. Let cool several hours until syrup firms up. Place in plate and store like other cookies.

MORE SWEETS AND DESSERTS:

FROM STRUDEL TO MANDEL *BROIT*

MOM'S CHANUKAH STRUDEL*

**Do not use low fat dairy products for this recipe.
Recipe needs fat in dough for best results.**

Dough
1 cup creamed cottage cheese (Use Breakstone's No Curds if you can get it.) Again, do not use low-fat products for this recipe. Recipe requires fat in dough for best results.

½ lb of butter—two sticks, softened (do not use margarine or light butter).

2 cups flour

Pinch of salt

Blend cottage cheese and butter; add flour and salt and mix well. Cover and place in refrigerator for 30 minutes. Remove. Let rest 10-15 minutes. Separate into 3 balls. Roll each ball very thin into a sort of rectangular shape on a floured board.

Filling
Melted butter

Sugar and cinnamon

Jams, orange marmalade, finely chopped apples

Chopped walnuts

Dates and/or raisins (I use golden raisins)

Mini or regular chocolate chips, optional

Poppy seeds, optional

(Continued next page)

Preheat oven to 350 degrees. Brush dough with melted butter and sprinkle with sugar and cinnamon. Spread jams and/or preserves or other ingredients; then add chopped walnuts and raisins. (I usually make two rolls with jams, raisins, dates, etc. and then another roll with chocolate chips, jams, nuts, etc.) Roll carefully using fine spatula to lift dough if needed.

Place rolls on lightly greased cookie sheet. Brush with slightly beaten egg and small amount of cold water. Sprinkle rolls lightly with mixture of sugar and cinnamon. (Can sprinkle chocolate roll with chocolate sprinkles to identify it from other one.) Bake in a 350 degree oven for 50 minutes or until lightly browned. Cool completely. Slice carefully about ½ inch thick to serve. Refrigerate if not using in next day or two. Can be frozen after being sliced and kept for a long time.

(Grandma Eisman made strudel but her recipe is not complete. I remember it was a very sweet strudel.)

GRANDMA EISMAN'S BANANA CAKE

David liked this when he was a kid.

½ cup Crisco (Grandma used this; I've used peanut or canola oil.)
1 ¼ cups sugar
2 egg yolks
2 bananas, mashed
2 cups flour
1 tsp baking powder
½ tsp baking soda
½ cup milk
2 egg whites
1 tsp vanilla
½ tsp salt
1 cup pecans chopped, optional

Preheat to 350 degrees. Blend sugar and oil. Separate yolks and whites. Add yolks and bananas and beat again. Sift baking powder and soda with flour. Alternate milk and dry ingredients. Fold in stiff egg whites. Bake in greased loaf pan for one hour at 350 degrees. Test doneness by inserting toothpick; if it comes out clean, cake is done. Cool completely before removing from pan.

GRANDMA EISMAN'S EASY SPONGE CAKE

This is the recipe I use for strawberry short cake.

6 eggs
1 cup flour
1 cup sugar
1½ tsp baking powder
Juice from ½ lemon
1 tsp vanilla

Preheat oven to 325 degrees. Blend all ingredients and mix well. Divide batter into two greased cake pans. (Grandma always baked this in one pan and cut through cake to make two layers. She said the cake was fluffier baked this way.) Bake two cake pans at 325 degrees for 35 minutes or until done. Insert toothpick to check for doneness. (If using one cake pan, bake for about one hour.)

To make strawberry short cake with drizzled chocolate center:

1 pint whipping cream
1 tablespoon powdered sugar
1 tsp vanilla
1 box strawberries
Hershey syrup

After cakes are done and cooled, remove from pans. Beat pint of whipped cream together with 1 tablespoon of powdered sugar and 1 teaspoon vanilla. Reserve whipped cream for top and sides of cake. Add cut-up strawberries to remaining whipping cream, gently blending, and spread over one cake. Drizzle Hershey Syrup onto top of whipped cream mixture. Place second cake over cream and chocolate. Frost top and sides of cake with generous amounts of whipped cream. Decorate with strawberries and few blueberries.

GRANDMA EISMAN'S COOKIES

David liked these cookies when he was a kid.
These cookies are quite firm and solid.

1 cup sugar
1 stick margarine
2 eggs
1/3-cup oil
2 tsp baking powder
1 tsp vanilla
Juice from one orange
4 cups flour
1 pack chocolate chips
Toppings of cinnamon, sugar and chopped nuts
Marmalade or strawberry jam

Preheat oven to 400 degrees. Cream sugar and margarine. Add oil and eggs, blending well. Add remaining ingredients except topping. Using teaspoon, scoop small amount of batter and dip into topping mixture placing each spoonful onto greased cookie sheet. Put small dollop of jam or jelly onto each cookie. You can also place one Hershey Kiss on a few cookies. (When I was a kid, we called Hershey Kisses chocolate "silver bells" because of its shape and silver wrapping.) Place in oven and bake at 400 degrees for 15 minutes.

AUNTIE ROSE'S *RUGELAH* RECIPE

Dough
½ cup warm water
2 yeast cakes
2 sticks margarine, melted
2 eggs
1 tsp vanilla
2 tsp sugar
2 ½ cups flour

Filling
1 cup sugar mixed with 1 tsp cinnamon to be divided into eight portions
Mixture of walnuts or pecans and raisins

Mix all dough ingredients together, adding 2 tablespoons flour if necessary. Place in refrigerator for 2 hours. Remove from refrigerator. Preheat oven to 350 degrees. Place on floured board and separate into 8 balls. Knead in about 2-3 tablespoons sugar and cinnamon mix into each ball. Roll out and divide into 8 triangles using extra flour for ease in handling. Sprinkle each with a bit of sugar and cinnamon mix, if desired. Add nuts and raisins to each triangle. Roll up starting at wide end. Bake on greased pan at 350 degrees for about 25 minutes.

EASY CHEESE CAKE
with CHOCOLATE CHIPS

Pam's favorite...People rave about this recipe because with the topping, it looks like it took hours to prepare!

1 cup graham cracker crumbs
3 tablespoons sugar
3 tablespoons margarine, melted
3 (8 oz) packages cream cheese, softened
¾ cups sugar
3 eggs
1 cup mini semi-sweet chocolate pieces
1 tsp vanilla
Strawberries, kiwi fruit, blueberries

Preheat oven to 450 degrees. Combine crumbs, sugar and margarine; press onto bottom of 9-inch springform pan. Combine cream cheese and sugar at medium speed and mix well. Add eggs, one at a time, mixing well after each; add vanilla. Blend in chocolate pieces and pour over crust. Bake at 450 degrees for 10 minutes; reduce oven temperature to 250 degrees and continue baking for 35 minutes. Test for doneness by inserting knife into center of cake. After cooling slightly, loosen cake from rim of pan. Cool completely before removing cake from pan. Chill. Before serving, decorate with strawberries, blueberries, kiwi fruit or other fresh fruit. Cake requires refrigeration. Makes 10 to 12 servings.

GRANDMA EISMAN'S COFFEE CAKE RECIPE

½ cup butter
1 cup sugar
2 eggs
2 cups flour
1 tsp baking soda
¼ tsp salt
1 cup sour cream
1 tsp vanilla

Topping
¼ cup granulated sugar
1 tsp cinnamon
1 cup raisins
1 cup pecans

Preheat oven to 350 degrees. Cream margarine and sugar; add eggs and sour cream and blend well. Add flour, other dry ingredients and vanilla. Blend well. Mix topping ingredients together and spread over batter. Bake at 350 for 45 minutes.

CREAM CHEESE CUPCAKES

3 (8 oz) packages of cream cheese
1 cup sugar
½ tsp vanilla
5 eggs
12 foil cupcake liners

Topping
1 cup sour cream
¼ cup sugar
¼ tsp vanilla

Preheat oven to 325 degrees. Blend softened cream cheese with sugar and vanilla until smooth. Add eggs and mix well. Fill foil cupcake liners in muffin tin about ¾ full—batter will rise. Cook in 325-degree oven for about 30 minutes or until a touch of light brown appears on some. Do not over bake. After removing from oven, let set 5 minutes. Mix topping ingredients and blend well. Top cakes with sour cream mixture. Top with dollop of colorful jam or jelly. Return to oven for about 5 minutes until sour cream mixture has set. Let cool several hours and refrigerate. Cupcakes are very fragile until cooled thoroughly. Can be frozen and then thawed in half hour and will keep in freezer for months. Makes 24 cupcakes.

MANDEL *BROIT* (Bread)

Looks and tastes like Biscotti

½ cup butter, softened
1 cup brown sugar, firmly packed
2 eggs
2¼ cups flour
1 tsp baking powder
½ tsp vanilla
½ tsp. almond extract
1 cup almonds, sliced, slivered or chopped
1 cup raisins

Preheat oven to 325 degrees. Cream together butter and sugar. Add eggs, flour, baking powder, vanilla, and almond extract. Stir in nuts. Shape into two long rolls on a greased cookie sheet. Bake for 30-35 minutes at 325 degrees. Slice each log into pieces. Leave on cookie sheet and brown in 400 degrees oven for 5-10 minutes.

Printed in the United States
63121LVS00004B/312

9 781424 148004